THE SONG OF SONGS WOMAN

A DANCE OF TWO ARMIES

"AT HIS FEET" SERIES

BOOK 2

Jane Carole Anderson

The Song of Songs Woman: A Dance of Two Armies
At His Feet Series—Book 2

by Jane Carole Anderson
editing by John R. D. Anderson
illustrations and cover art by Jane Carole Anderson

Bible abbreviations used:

AMP, Amplified Bible

ASV, American Standard Version

KJV, King James Version

NASB, New American Standard Version

ISBN 978-0-9769835-6-9

Typographical changes have been made to some Bible verses to fit with the style of this publication.

Scripture quotations taken from the Amplified® Bible (AMP), Copyright © 2015 by The Lockman Foundation. Used by permission.

Scripture quotations taken from the New American Standard Bible® (NASB), Copyright © 1960, 1962, 1963, 1968, 1971, 1972, 1973, 1975, 1977, 1995 by The Lockman Foundation. Used by permission.

Protus
Publications
LemonsToGrapes.com

DEDICATION

This book is dedicated to my six granddaughters: Sarah, Hannah, Abigail, Claire, Madison, and Naomi. It is my hope and prayer that what they will learn from these pages will be written in their hearts by the Spirit of God and that it will help them become lovers of Jesus Christ and spiritual warriors in His kingdom. May they be inspired to spend their lives making themselves ready, and helping others become ready, for the Bridegroom's soon coming!

TABLE OF CONTENTS

MY HEARTFELT THANKS TO ...

My husband, John, for his loving support, his invaluable help in authoring, and his faithful editing.

Lanell Allen, Karen Johnson, and Kay Leatherman for their wonderful friendship and for their combined many years of fellowship and prayer about matters covered in this book. I also thank them for their invaluable content reviews and helpful editing.

Other faithful Christian women I have been privileged to know over the years, for their inspirational stories and testimonies about how God has strengthened them and helped them become women of *chayil*.

My two sons and their wives for six wonderful granddaughters that have been a source of constant inspiration and motivation in the writing of this book.

The Author and Finisher of our faith, Who, by causing all things to work together for good, is the One who is ultimately responsible for this publication and the One I thank most of all.

AT HIS FEET

This book is one in a series entitled, "At His Feet," by Jane Carole Anderson. The series contains some of what Jane has learned sitting at the feet of Jesus with her Bible.

When she was twenty-five years old, Jane had her first experience of God teaching her from His Word. A few years later, she was openly denounced by a Christian leader and told that a woman could not get revelation from the Bible. As a result, she was confused and stopped reading her Bible for a long period of time. After Jesus healed her heart, she began to spend time again at His feet. What she has learned from His Word reminds me of the following stanza from a hymn:

> We limit not the truth of God
> To our poor reach of mind,
> By notions of our day and sect,
> Crude, partial and confined.
> Now let a new and better hope
> Within our hearts be stirred:
> The Lord hath yet more light and truth
> To break forth from His word.

> — George Rawson (1807–1889)

Readers can, of course, make up their own minds about Jane's inspiration. I think that the insights from the Holy Word of God that Jane has passed on to us in this writing speak well of both her and her teacher.

— John R. D. Anderson

WRITING CONVENTIONS

Footnotes: Footnotes appear at the end of the paragraphs in which they occur.

References: References to Bushnell are to the paragraphs in her book, *God's Word to Women: One Hundred Bible Studies on Woman's Place in the Church and Home*. Minneapolis: Christians for Biblical Equality, 2003.

Typography: Brackets and italic font that normally indicate supplied words in some Bible versions have been removed so as not to distract from the poetic impact of the Song of Songs. Also, the format of all Bible versions has been unified to appear as poetry.

Writer's Comments: Writer's comments, set in italic type, are interjected throughout the author's presentation of the Song of Songs story to provide information and explanation related to her narrative.

Foreword

SONG OF SONGS (OR SONG OF SOLOMON) is a book in the Bible that is wonderful yet puzzling. Are the two main persons in it married or lovers, or are they just courting? Which words are his, and which are hers? Who are the others that speak at intervals during the narrative? These kinds of questions always presented themselves whenever I tried to read this book. I didn't pay much attention to them except for a few times when I was awakened in the middle of the night with the following verse in my mind:

> A garden enclosed is my sister, my spouse;
> A spring shut up, a fountain sealed. (Song 4:12, KJV)

When this happened, I looked up the verse, read its context, and then read through the whole book. I would puzzle over it, pray about it, and eventually set aside my unanswered questions for another day.

I never understood what God wanted me to hear through this verse until the summer of 2013. While spending time preparing for a women's retreat that fall, the Lord unexpectedly began a summer-long visit with me in Song of Songs. After awakening with the above verse early that summer, I began to read through the book again; but, this time, it was different. The doors of my understanding started to swing open. The idea was set into my mind that what I had learned from a book by Katharine Bushnell, *God's Word to Women,* was a key to answering some of the questions this book posed for me. I asked the Lord that if, indeed, He was talking to me about Song of Songs, He would not give up on me and would help me until I realized what He wanted me to understand.

A Mare Among Stallions

First of all, realizing that there were many and varied interpretations of this book available, I noted that a number had been written by men who saw much of the imagery in this book to be about sex. I was not convinced as to the validity or applicability of such a view. It occurred to me that the weight given to sexual imagery might actually fog the view God wanted to give us. A comment about mares and stallions that I read in the NET Bible on Song of Songs 1:9 on the phrase, "among the chariot-horses," illustrates my point:

> Heb "among the chariot-horses" or "among the chariots." ... Pope offers the best explanation of this enigmatic picture: "A crucial consideration overlooked by commentators is the well-attested fact that Pharaoh's chariots, like other chariotry in antiquity, were not drawn by a mare or mares but by stallions hitched in pairs. This bit of intelligence radically alters the usual understanding of the verse and dispels the notion that there is a grammatical incongruity, which needs harmonizing. The juxtaposition is between a single mare and a plurality of stallions and it requires only a modicum of what is called 'horse sense' to appreciate the thrust of the comparison. The situation envisaged is illustrated by the famous incident in one of the campaigns of Thutmose III against Qadesh. On his tomb at Thebes, the Egyptian soldier Amenemheb relates how the Prince of Qadesh sent forth a swift mare, which entered among the army. But Amenemheb ran after her on foot and with his dagger ripped open her belly, cut off her tail, and presented it to the king, thus preventing a debacle before the excited stallions could take out after the mare." (Song 1:9, NET, note 49)

In other words, "O my beloved, you are like a mare among Pharaoh's stallions" (Song, 1:9, NET) was understood to mean that she was sexually exciting like a mare in Pharaoh's army would be, causing all the stallions to chase after her. The interpretation offered here is a rather crude, sexual one and didn't, in my opinion, contribute much in the way of inspiration or revelation from God. The thought became firmly lodged in my mind that the reason men had not been able with convincing clarity to explain the narrative and unlock all the symbolism in Song of Songs was that they did not have adequate input from women who could offer female perspectives on the story.

The Door Is Open

It occurred to me that the uncertain or incomplete sound of the male expositions and interpretations was actually an invitation for another female perspective, and it was one that I should accept. As I began to study, pray, and write, I took into consideration information I had already learned from male-authored commentaries; however, I decided to reserve for later use any commentaries that I had not examined yet. I had asked the Lord to give me light and decided I would first give the Spirit opportunity to teach me and guide me. I believe my prayer for light and instruction was answered to some degree, and believe that the Lord enabled me to make a good beginning with some good discoveries that provide more understanding of this book.

During the weeks that followed, I felt like there was a circle of light in my understanding; and, each time I stepped into it, it increased in brightness by degrees like the dawning grows into morning, until I was standing in the full light of day and the book was no longer a mystery to me.

In Song of Songs, the Spirit of God uses inspired poetic writing to capture the symbolic story of love between Solomon and a woman. Some say that the woman symbolizes the the church and also symbolizes an individual believer. I agree with both of these; however, in addition, I now see a third thing she symbolizes, and that is godly women throughout time. In other words, the Song of Songs story portrays the interactions between God and godly women, individually, collectively, and historically, from the time in the Garden of Eden to the second coming of Christ. This view complements the other two symbolisms. From beginning to end, the story paints a picture of the pathway that believers travel to become God's woman of *chayil*.[1] It portrays woman in a way that redefines our traditionally held views of womankind, and it does so for the better. The woman that emerges at the end of the Song of Songs is one that matches with the character, capability, and beauty of the wonderful woman that emerges at the end of the Bible, the bride of Christ.

---

[1] Pronounced khah'-yil. "... the Hebrew word cha-yil (חַ֫יִל) ... occurs 242 times in the Old Testament. It is translated 'army' and 'war' 58 times; 'host' and 'forces' 43 times; 'might' or 'power' 16 times; 'goods,' 'riches,' 'substance' and 'wealth' in all 31 times; 'band of soldiers,' 'band of men,' 'company,' and 'train' once each; 'activity' once; 'valor' 28 times; 'strength' 11 times: these are all noun forms. The word is often translated as an adjective or adverb. It is translated 'valiant' and 'valiantly' 35 times; 'strong' 6 times; 'able' 4 times; 'worthily' once and 'worthy' once. We have now given you the complete list of the various renderings of this word excepting four instances in which the word is used in describing a woman" (Bushnell, para. 624). In these four instances, the word is translated "virtue" or "virtuous." Possibly the translators found it difficult to ascribe such a strong word to women.

What I have learned has brought greater clarity to the interpretation that the Song of Songs woman is the bride of Christ. It tells something wonderful about what kind of woman this bride is and shows what the individual believers who compose her look like. This woman begins as one who is weak, suppressed, bound, defeated, and without any influence; but, after she encounters Solomon and is drawn by his unique and wonderful love for her in her poor condition, and after she continues to pursue him and overcome great difficulties as she learns to trust him, she becomes a strong, capable, long-suffering, victorious, wealthy, and very influential woman!

I found, in the simple fact of the existence of this book, an expression of the tender, loving, heart of God toward all His seeking believers, and in particular, women believers. It displays His keen awareness of what they have suffered at the hands of God's enemy and His faithfulness to bring them to a place of freedom, peace, victory, joy, and blessing. A clear picture of this path is observable in the plight and journey of godly women who have suffered for centuries, since the time of the fall of mankind—the time when God pronounced the role woman would play in bringing forth the seed of woman for defeating God's enemy. God-fearing women have suffered particular persecution because God's enemy has sought to thwart God's promise of providing a victorious seed that would be born of woman. The Song of Songs story exemplifies the truth that all who will live godly in Christ Jesus will suffer persecution (2 Tim. 3:12); and, that those who suffer such, after a little while, God will perfect, establish, settle, and strengthen (2 Pet. 5:10).

Song of Songs itself is a perfectly fitting piece of love poetry set near the center of the Bible. It is a book which tells the greatest love story ever told and is a Song of all songs. The story has the ability to light the fire of holy love for Christ in the hearts of all who read it, and also to fuel their desire to stand strong and fight the battle of faith that believers are called to fight, not being stopped by any kind of suffering.

My conscious love for the Lord and my intimacy with Him grew immensely during my summer journey through Song of Songs. I was strengthened to stand one with Him, the true lover of my soul, without counting the cost to myself. I was empowered to fearlessly fight the battle, in company with many others, who by faith are wielding the sword of the Spirit, the Word of truth, and are overcoming the evil one, knowing that soon we will be enjoying for all eternity our beloved bridegroom, Christ.

Introduction: Behind the Scenes

Who is the Woman?

SONG OF SONGS IS AN ALLEGORY that needs interpretation. Interpretation is easier when the background of a composition is understood, so I sought to discover a plausible historical story in the Bible that would fit with Song of Songs. At the time the Lord turned my attention to Song of Songs, I had just reached this place in my daily Bible reading:

> 1 Now King David was old, advanced in age; and they covered him with clothes, but he could not keep warm. 2 So his servants said to him, "Let them seek a young virgin for my lord the king, and let her attend the king and become his nurse; and let her lie in your bosom, that my lord the king may keep warm." 3 So they searched for a beautiful girl throughout all the territory of Israel, and found Abishag the Shunammite, and brought her to the king. 4 The girl was very beautiful; and she became the king's nurse and served him, but the king did not cohabit with her. (1 Kings 1:1–4, NASB)

I asked myself, "Is it possible that the woman in Song of Songs was Abishag? Couldn't Solomon, the son of David, have met and fallen in love with the beautiful, young Abishag while she was living in David's house, taking care of his needs in old age?" 1st Kings 1:4 shows that she did not lose her virginity with David, so she would have remained eligible for Solomon's pursuit. This would be highly likely considering the Bible says she was *very beautiful.* Had God allowed this little piece of information about Abishag's virginity to be in the Holy Word as a clue to the identity of the woman in Song of Songs so that any who sought to discover her identity might find it?

I did a Bible study looking for any other evidence and for any other characters that may have played a part in the actual story behind the scenes during the time that

Song of Songs was written. Then, from my findings, I constructed a possible and plausible background story. I filled in various details of this constructed narrative by using my understanding of relevant Bible accounts, my understanding of people in general, my understanding of the devil, my understanding of the Lord, and my understanding of their various interrelationships. Of course, I had to take some license in doing this, so I make no claim that the story I present is the actual one; but, I do believe that my narrative, and my interpretation which is based on it, is every bit as feasible as some of the other interpretations that I have read. In regard to unlocking Song of Song's symbolism, I believe my interpretation turns out to be, as Katharine Bushnell says about the harmony of the Scriptures, "a fit all around."

A Brief Overview of Biblical Facts that Support My Background Story

This section contains a brief overview of biblical facts that support the background for the story that I develop in this book. (For more supporting details, see the appendix.)

I believe, as many scholars do, that "King Lemuel" in Proverbs 31:1 is King Solomon. Solomon was taught by his mother, Bathsheba, and learned what he wrote in Proverbs 31 from her. What she taught him shows her belief that a woman should be strong and valorous, something she learned through her own life experience— especially through her own failure as a woman with King David. Proverbs 31 shows Bathsheba's desire for the son of her vows to properly regard and relate to women, and to appreciate and desire for a wife a woman who was strong, capable, and even assertive in matters of morality, provision, and protection of her loved ones. It also shows that Solomon embraced his mother's teaching (Prov. 31:1–2; 10–30).

The events of 1st Kings 1:1–5 took place not long after Abishag had come to the palace. At that time, Adonijah, Solomon's older half brother, realized that King

David was about to die, and he influenced some of David's men to follow him and crown him king. Adonijah invited all his brothers to his coronation, but he excluded, among others, Solomon and Nathan the prophet.

Nathan then warned Bathsheba about Adonijah's self-crowning and advised her how to tell David about it. When Bathsheba informed King David, Abishag was present to hear that Adonijah might harm Bathsheba and Solomon. Nathan came to David after Bathsheba talked to him, and he confirmed her words to David (1 Kings 1:11–21).

David, then, took steps to have Solomon crowned king (1 Kings 1:28–40). When Adonijah heard this, he feared for his life, and he sought and obtained Solomon's mercy. Solomon let him live with the warning that, if wickedness was ever found in him, he would die. (1 Kings 1:41–53).

Shortly after this, David died. Adonijah appeared on scene again and used Bathsheba to try and trap Solomon into giving Abishag to Adonijah as his wife. Solomon, who had promised his mother to give her whatever she asked before he heard her request, avoided fulfilling his promise to her by killing Adonijah for his wicked trap, just as he had said he would do if he found wickedness in Adonijah (1 Kings 2:10–25). It is striking that when Adonijah tried to steal the kingdom, Solomon spared Adonijah's life; but, when Adonijah tried to take Abishag as his wife, Solomon had him killed!

> For love is strong as death;
> Jealousy is cruel as Sheol (Song 8:6, ASV)

With this background in mind, I began my interpretation of Song of Songs with the premise that the woman in Song of Songs was Abishag from Shunem. Ultimately, I concluded that both Abishag and the story surrounding her in the Bible were an excellent fit for interpreting Song of Songs—so excellent in fact that I will never again be able to see the Song of Songs woman as any other than Abishag. She was an excellent fit, not only for interpretation, but also for application.

The book begins with the woman's words, so some commentators have suggested that the book may have been composed by a woman. I began my reading and studying as if this were the case. Eventually, I realized that there is a strong possibility that Abishag, under the inspiration of the Spirit, and in collaboration with Solomon, composed the poetry in remembrance of their unique courtship. My interpretation offers evidence for this possibility.

Chapter 1: A Time of Love—The Beginning (Song 1:1–2:6)

THE OPENING VERSES OF SONG OF SONGS describe the beginning of love between Solomon and Abishag.

NARRATOR speaks:

1 The Song of songs, which is Solomon's. (KJV)

ABISHAG speaks:

2 Let him kiss me with the kisses of his mouth;

For thy love is better than wine. (KJV)

3 Thine oils have a goodly fragrance;

Thy name is as oil poured forth;

Therefore do the virgins love thee. (ASV)

4 Draw me; we will run after thee:

The king hath brought me into his chambers;

We will be glad and rejoice in thee; (KJV)

We will make mention of thy love more than of wine:

Rightly do they love thee. (ASV)

ABISHAG continues:

5 I am black, but comely,

Oh ye daughters of Jerusalem,

As the tents of Kedar,

As the curtains of Solomon. (KJV)

6 Look not upon me, because I am swarthy,

Because the sun hath scorched me.

My mother's sons were incensed against me;

They made me keeper of the vineyards;

But mine own vineyard have I not kept. (ASV)

Song of Songs opens with Abishag speaking. She has fallen in love with Solomon and is ready to let him kiss her. She is in the King's house where she can have wine when she wishes, but she delights more in hearing Solomon's name. It flows over her like oil. When she hears his name, it usually means he is near, he is coming, and she will get to see him. She has decided to allow him to kiss her. She says his love is better than wine, because it is a very special kind of love, one she has never known before.

The words "let him" are important, showing it is her choice to let him kiss her. As Solomon loved Abishag, God already loves us with a never failing love, yet we cannot know the sweetness of that love if we do not let Him show His love to us. It is our choice to make, and He waits patiently for us to make it.

She wants Solomon to call her away to see him. She has been talking to the daughters of Jerusalem about his wonderful and kind love. From just hearing about him, they also are attracted to him.

Abishag remembers how she came to the palace and to the King's bedchamber.

Considering the holiness of God and His commandments for us to also be holy, it is hard to understand how this woman would be brought so quickly (by Song 4:1) into Solomon's chambers, referring to his apartment or bed chamber. This sounds like she was immediately sexually intimate with him. This seems to be a misfit in this love story, happening outside of marriage and without courtship and preparation; however, if this woman is Abishag, the problem is easily cleared up. The writer was not referring to Solomon's chambers, but to King David's chambers, because Abishag was brought to sleep with King David in order to keep his old flesh warm.

Abishag had been brought from a village in northern Israel named Shunem to King David's palace to keep him warm. This was hard for her because she had to give up her whole life and the future possibility of a normal marriage and family. She realized that there was a reason they wanted to find a beautiful virgin, and she didn't like what this was going to mean for her. Once in the palace, she did get into bed with King David to keep him warm, but she refused to lose her virginity. She was brave enough to risk drawing a line there.

Bathsheba, David's aged wife, was naturally bothered by the fact that a beautiful young woman was going to be sleeping with her husband at night, but she was pleased to learn by Abishag's unexpected stand what kind of woman she was—she was a woman of *chayil*, one who was strong enough to do the right thing in the face of a very difficult situation with her king. Bathsheba knew only too well by now how she herself had not done the right thing many years before when David had brought her to his bedchamber.

The fact that Abishag was treated basically as if she was no more than a warm piece of flesh to keep an old king warm shows a lot about how women in the culture of David's day were viewed. The servants had suggested finding a "young virgin" for David. (Apparently, this seemed to be a perfectly normal suggestion to them.) Then, they had searched throughout the land of Israel for a fair virgin, found Abishag, and brought her to sleep with David. The fact that she was "brought" does not sound like she was given a choice. She had to leave her home and family, give up her own life, come to the palace, and press her flesh against David's, who was, until that day, a stranger to her. This seems to be a rather personally demeaning job. This whole scenario begs the question: Why did David need a beautiful young virgin? If his need was for warmth, why not a young eunuch? Why did it have to be a woman who was young and beautiful?

The Bible says plainly that David did not have sexual relations with Abishag (1 Kings 1:4); so, in that regard, he treated her with respect. It is possible, however, that this is recorded because Abishag refused him, as my narrative says. Then, David, possibly remembering what he had done to Bathsheba, respected Abishag's wishes. Not only was Abishag's person disregarded in this matter, so was Bathsheba's. Neither of these women seems to have had much say in the decision to bring Abishag. The culture dictated the norm; and, regardless of how they really felt about it, women typically went along with the norm and found ways to conform and cope. I think that Abishag drew the line on being used in such a way by an old king. If so, we can hear her voice in the Bible verse that says that David did not have sex with her. I think it interesting that the Bible tells us this fact. Maybe it was a clue left by the Holy Spirit for anyone who might wonder if the Song of Songs' woman was Abishag. At least they would know that she was eligible to be Solomon's wife because she had not been sexually involved with David.

In this demeaning situation, Abishag meets Solomon. He falls in love with her; but, true to the teaching of his mother with regard to women, he is careful to not make her feel uncomfortable, uneasy, or disrespected. He behaves in a way that lets her see his true character, including the respect that he has for women. She sees him as upright.

From a woman's perspective, Abishag could have spoken such words of adoration and love for Solomon as found in Song of Songs only if she had been truly loved and treated with respect and care by him. To a woman, this book is not about physical intimacy, it is about the discovery of true love. Solomon eventually had many wives and clearly was not practicing what his mother had taught him, so Abishag may have been his first love; and, their love began at a time when he had not yet forsaken his mother's law, which contained warnings about seductive women (Prov. 1:8, 6:20).

The first one in Song of Songs to make a move of love toward the other is the woman. She has not been forced to accept Solomon; rather, he has behaved in a way to win her heart. She may have been resistant at first because, as we shortly will learn, her past experience with males was not good. She has become convinced that Solomon is different. When she says concerning Solomon, "the upright love thee," she is testifying that she has found him to be an upright man whom upright persons love. She is an upright woman, and she has grown to love him.

Abishag has met and become friends with some of the daughters of Jerusalem. She explains to them why her skin is black. She is ashamed of this and tells them not to look at her. Her skin is black because the sun darkened it when she was keeping vineyards. She now confesses that it was her mother's sons, her brothers, who were responsible for this. They were angry with her and made her keep the vineyards. She tells her women friends in Jerusalem that, because of this, she did not keep her own vineyard. This is an unpleasant memory for her.

Concerning the phrase, "my mother's sons," some translations say, "my mother's children"; but, the Hebrew word used here is "ben," which usually means "son" (Vine, H1121)."My mother's sons" could symbolize fallen males in the line of Cain, the serpent's seed. Such men are used by the devil to persecute, even kill, godly people. Such men are also used to thwart and afflict godly women. They rule over women and make them take care of other vineyards than their own. Women have been mistreated by such angry males throughout both world and church history. The sun is the heat that comes while being forced to take care of another's vineyard like a slave, rather than one's own. A vineyard, in the Old Testament, represents one's inheritance. Naboth would not sell his vineyard to Ahab because it was his inheritance, and he knew it would be wrong for him to sell it (1 Kings 21:2–3). Women have become changed (blackened) by this kind of mistreatment.

Solomon was not like Abishag's angry brothers. Because of the hurt by her brothers, she may have had a basic distrust of men. In the palace, observing Solomon, she had begun to see that he was a different sort of man. Over time, she had initiated more intimate conversations with him, let down her guard, and opened her heart to him.

ABISHAG continues:

7 Tell me, O thou whom my soul loveth,

Where thou feedest thy flock,

Where thou makest it to rest at noon:

For why should I be as one that is veiled

Beside the flocks of thy companions? (ASV)

SOLOMON speaks:

8 If thou know not, O thou fairest among women,

Go thy way forth by the footsteps of the flock,

And feed thy kids beside the shepherds' tents. (KJV)

9 I have compared thee, O my love,

To a steed in Pharaoh's chariots. (ASV)

10 Thy cheeks are comely with plaits of hair,

Thy neck with strings of jewels. (ASV)

11 We will make thee plaits of gold

With studs of silver. (ASV)

Abishag and Solomon have begun to meet secretly in the gardens and other places. He has invited her to a rendezvous with him when he goes to see his flocks. She has told him that she loves him. She has asked him to clarify where he feeds his flocks. She wanted to know where his flocks were so that she could avoid veiling herself to hide her beauty. Her beauty could put her in danger of the male shepherds as she goes looking for his flock among the flocks of his friends.

To veil herself could make her look like a prostitute, says one commentator. Maybe she is tired of having to hide who she really is with a veil in order to keep from being abused by men. This could be symbolic of many women who have learned that if they allow their spiritual abilities and gifts, their spiritual beauty, to be seen, they may suffer for it.

Solomon had understood the reason for her question and told her exactly what to do to be safe. He told her to take some of the young female goats from the king's stock and graze them in a place near the other shepherds. In this way, she would appear to be a shepherdess and not stand out as she would if she went walking alone. He would be able to look for her small female goat flock and find her.

Solomon can hardly wait to be alone with her. He has confessed his love for her and told her how he sees her. By this time, he has heard that she refused to become one of David's concubines; and, because of this, Solomon sees her like a strong mare, so strong that he compares her to one of the stallions that pulls Pharaoh's chariots, wearing war garb. He sees her strength as something beautiful and wants to make her strength more beautiful by adorning her with gold, silver, and jewels. His description acknowledges her as a woman of *chayil,* the kind of woman that his mother taught him to appreciate and find for himself.

ABISHAG thinks:

12 While the king sat at his table,

My spikenard sent forth its fragrance. (ASV)

13 My beloved is unto me as a bundle of myrrh,

That lieth betwixt my breasts. (ASV)

14 My beloved is unto me as a cluster of henna-flowers

In the vineyards of En-gedi. (ASV)

While sitting at David's table, Abishag is contemplating Solomon and is anticipating their next meeting. She will smell as spikenard for him, and he will be like a bundle of myrrh to her. She dreams of what it would be for him to lie all night between her breasts and dreams that such a time will come. Thinking about when she has met him before in secret in the gardens nearby, she remembers him like a cluster of camphire in the vineyards of Engedi. Solomon is to her like a plant she has seen in a place of rest and refuge for the persecuted in Engedi (the place where David was persecuted by Saul). She prepares to tell him again how fair he is. She will tell him he has eyes like doves. She remembers how they rested together in the garden in secret and speaks to herself about the garden like it was their secret home with a green grass bed and a ceiling made of tree branches, cedar, and fir. When they meet, she will tell him that she considers herself to be no more than a rose or lily that grows in low valleys.

ABISHAG speaks:

15 Behold, thou art fair, my love;

Behold thou art fair;

Thine eyes are as doves. (ASV)

16 Behold, thou art fair, my beloved, yea, pleasant:

Also our couch is green. (ASV)

17 The beams of our house are cedars,

And our rafters are firs. (ASV)

2:1 I am a rose of Sharon,

A lily of the valleys. (ASV)

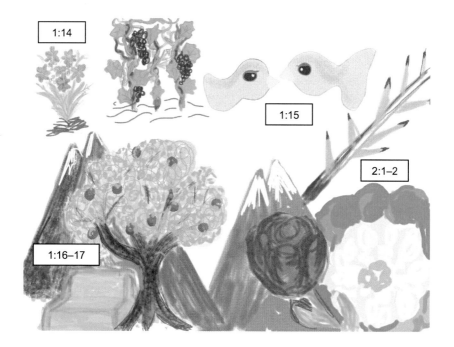

SOLOMON speaks:

2 As a lily among thorns,

So is my love among the daughters. (ASV)

He gently improves her low assessment of herself by saying that he sees her as a lily among thorns, referring to other women who are not as beautiful as she is, and who do not love singly, as she does. He sees her, when compared with the other daughters, like a lily among thorns.

The abundance of garden imagery in Song of Songs supports the idea that they met often in gardens. It is also reminiscent of mankind being in a garden setting with God in the beginning. One commentator says that doves' eyes may refer to the warmth of doves mating. I think it may refer to the fact that doves mate for life; hence, he sees beauty in the fact that she has eyes only for him.

Abishag refers to Solomon in the second person (you, your) in chapter 1, then she changes to speak about him in third person (he, his) throughout most of the Song until the end. Then she switches back to the more personal second person. Solomon typically speaks to her in second person throughout the story.

ABISHAG speaks:

3 As the apple-tree among the trees of the wood,

So is my beloved among the sons.

I sat down under his shadow with great delight,

And his fruit was sweet to my taste. (ASV)

4 He brought me to the banqueting-house,

And his banner over me was love. (ASV)

She also makes a comparison between him and other males. He is a beautiful apple tree, one that shields her from the burning sun and supplies her with food. She loves to sit under the shadow he makes for her and eat what he provides for her. Other men (her mother's sons) have not shaded her but put her in the fields under the sun that scorched her. Her beloved is different.

She describes, possibly to some daughters of Jerusalem, how she sat under Solomon's shade. He was a protection for her from the hot sun. She found his treatment delightful. He brought her to his family's house of wine and declared his love for her. (The Hebrew word that is translated "banqueting" is the usual word for fermented grape and is usually rendered "wine" [Vine, H3196].)

2:5

2:6

ABISHAG continues:

5 Stay ye me with raisins, refresh me with apples;

For I am sick from love. (ASV)

6 His left hand is under my head,

And his right hand doth embrace me. (ASV)

Feeling weak with love, she eats some food. She describes for the daughters how he embraces her, and then she tells them not to wake him for he had fallen asleep in the garden where they were together. She is always attentively listening for his voice and watching for signs of his coming. As soon as she hears his voice, she points this out to others.

Let's look at some of the symbolism in my interpretation of Song of Songs thus far: David is a type of Christ as a man on the earth; Solomon is a type of Christ reigning in victory. Abishag ministering to David before he dies, and taking care of his flesh, may represent the women who ministered to Christ when He was in the flesh. While with Christ, these women, like Abishag, were getting to know the One who, after His death on the cross, would become the King in resurrection. These women fell in love with Christ because of the kind of man He was, different than all the other men they had known. All of Abishag's assessment of Solomon thus far may symbolize the way women saw Jesus when He was in the flesh. Jesus treated them wonderfully, unlike other men of their day, especially religious ones. Also, just as Abishag does after David's death, these women transitioned from taking care of Christ in the flesh to loving Him as the King in resurrection.

If Abishag ministering to David symbolizes the women who were with Christ at the time of His first coming, then we can consider the possibility that Abishag's comment about her mother's sons being angry with her symbolizes the situation on the earth at the time of Christ with respect to how Jewish women were treated by Jewish men. These women were living under the teachings of the Jewish oral law which had developed during the Days of Mingling.[2] These women suffered mistreatment by their brothers, men who were living out the fallen Adamic nature and who were, as Jesus said, "of their father the devil" (John 8:44) and were the seed of the serpent mentioned in Genesis 3. They treated women like slaves in vineyards, didn't allow them to take care of their own inheritance, and blackened their skin by this kind of oppression and suppression. It may also refer to the situation of Jewish women in Old Testament times before Christ came. For example, women were demeaned and disrespected by having to be one of multiple wives and concubines who were ruled over by one husband.

---

[2] During the four hundred years between the last Old Testament writing and the first New Testament writing, the rabbis' teachings were responsible for the subjugation of women. During those years, referred to as the "Days of Mingling," the Jews were seeking acceptance by the Greeks. Corrupt rabbis allowed Greek mythology and practices to influence their beliefs and teachings. For example, the Greek myth of Pandora's box was overlaid on the story of Eve and the forbidden fruit. They developed an oral tradition that was different from the teachings of the Old Testament, and set it forth as truth. This is what Jesus spoke strongly against when He came. By then, the oral tradition had become known as the oral law, and it was later written down and is known today as the Talmud. Perverted teachings about women in the Talmud are at the root of wrong beliefs about women which are still held today. These teachings were used by the Judaizers (the Jews who accepted Christ) to influence and persuade the early church to believe things that were not in God's Word (Bushnell, paras. 86–87).

In my interpretation, I have said that the king whom Abishag kept warm was King David. David was a type of Christ, as one who fought the battle with God's enemies and won the victory. He, however, did not build the temple. It was built by Solomon who is also a type of Christ, reigning in his heavenly kingdom. Therefore, I suggest that in Song of Songs, the events that happened while King David was still alive (needing warmth for his health) symbolically refer to events in the Old Testament period. Events that happened after David died and Solomon was enthroned symbolize the New Testament period, the time after Christ's death and resurrection, when Christ was made both Lord and Christ by God (Acts 2:36). Also, in the same way that Abishag was beaten by watchmen in the streets of the city after Solomon was made king, so New Testament women have been mistreated by their Christian brothers after the time that Christ was enthroned.

Chapter 2: A Time of Fear—Love is Threatened (Song 2:7-3:4)

A BISHAG CONTINUES SPEAKING with further expressions of new love, but her love is about to turn to fear.

7 I adjure you, O daughters of Jerusalem,

By the roes, or by the hinds of the field,

That ye stir not up, nor awake my love,

Until he please. (ASV)

The timing of the mention of the daughters of Jerusalem is noteworthy. Their appearance seems to function like a pause, showing the reader that there is a break in time in the story line.

8 Listen! My beloved!

Behold, he is coming,

Climbing on the mountains,

Leaping on the hills! (NASB)

9 My beloved is like a gazelle or a young stag.

Behold, he is standing behind our wall,

He is looking through the windows,

He is peering through the lattice. (NASB)

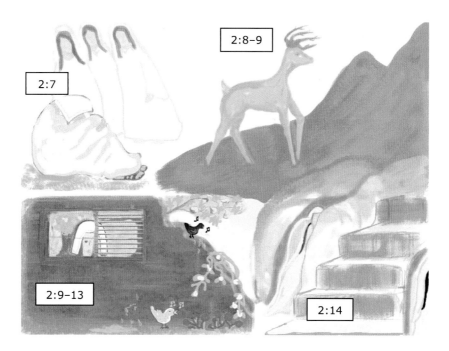

SOLOMON speaks:

10 My beloved responded and said to me,

"Arise, my darling, my beautiful one,

And come along. (NASB)

11 "For behold, the winter is past,

The rain is over and gone. (NASB)

12 "The flowers have already appeared in the land;

The time has arrived for pruning the vines,

And the voice of the turtledove has been heard in our land. (NASB)

13 "The fig tree has ripened its figs,

And the vines in blossom have given forth their fragrance.

Arise, my darling, my beautiful one,

And come along!" (NASB)

ABISHAG speaks:

14 "O my dove, that art in the clefts of the rock,

In the secret places of the stairs,

Let me see thy countenance,

Let me hear thy voice;

For sweet is thy voice, and thy countenance is comely. (KJV)

From this point forward, we will see that something has happened which has caused Abishag to feel reluctant to be with Solomon. Prior to this, their communication had been open and wonderful. Now, she is entering a time of fear in which her love for him is threatened. This period of trials takes place when they are separated from each other.

Abishag hears Solomon's voice in the early morning like a roe or young hart skipping on the mountains, coming to see and talk with her. He comes to the part of the palace where Abishag is staying. He is outside, hiding behind a wall, one they have labeled "our wall," maybe because they have met there often. He looks through the windows and shows himself through the lattices, hoping to be seen by her, to get her attention.

It has been winter, and Abishag has had to spend more time with King David to keep him warm. She and Solomon have not seen much of each other. She hears him calling her to come with him, telling her that winter is over. They can meet again in the gardens. He entices her with a description of the blooming garden. During the winter, they have been meeting in the clefts of rocks in the mountains or in secret places of the staircases of David's house, instead of in the gardens, but now he wants to see her in the garden. He sounds happy to be able to see her in such a setting again.

She tells him that she loves hearing his voice and seeing his face. She acknowledges it would be good to see him in the garden again, but she doesn't come out.

SOLOMON speaks:

15 "Catch the foxes for us,

The little foxes that are ruining the vineyards,

While our vineyards are in blossom." (NASB)

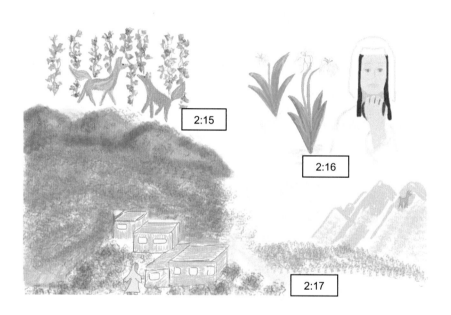

ABISHAG speaks:

16 My beloved is mine, and I am his;

He pastures his flock among the lilies. (NASB)

17 Until the cool of the day when the shadows flee away,

Turn, my beloved, and be like a gazelle

Or a young stag on the mountains of Bether. (NASB)

He has a very good excuse to ask her to come—it is time to take care of the vineyards and catch the little foxes that are spoiling the blooms.

What are the little foxes? The NET Bible note on this passage says:

> The term "foxes" is used metaphorically. Foxes are always spoken of in a negative light in the OT and in the ancient world were particularly associated with their destructive tendencies with regard to vineyards (Judg. 15:4; Ne 4:3; Ps 63:10; La 5:18; Eze 13:4). The description of these foxes as being destructive here seems to confirm that this is the point of comparison in mind. In ancient Near Eastern love literature it was common to use wild animals to symbolize potential problems which could separate lovers and destroy their love. For instance, in Egyptian love songs it is the crocodile, rather than the foxes, which were used as figures for obstacles which might threaten a couple's love. Here the "foxes" are probably used figuratively to represent potentially destructive problems which could destroy their romantic relationship and which could hinder it from ripening into marriage (NET Bible Notes).

Based on the background story in the Bible during the time of Abishag and Solomon, I believe that the little foxes that are threatening their relationship are problems that have emerged because Adonijah has made himself King.

Solomon wants to tell her that problems caused by Adonijah's actions are just little foxes that want to spoil their blooming vine of love—and that they won't succeed. Solomon has learned that David is going to make him king, and he wants to tell Abishag because it means, as King, he can put Adonijah out of the picture and marry Abishag. But he doesn't get the opportunity to tell her.

This is the first time Abishag does not respond to Solomon when he calls her to come out and be with him in the early morning shadows. She reminds herself how much she loves him and what she has learned about him and his loving kindness, and then she tells him to go away until day breaks and there are no shadows. She tells him to flee to the mountains of Bether, indicating she believes there is danger.

According to one commentary, there are no mountains of Bether in Israel, so this should be understood by the meaning of the word "Bether," which is "separation."

For her to send him away urgently is a change. She has always gone with him before. But now she is frightened by what she was present to overhear when Bathsheba and Nathan talked to David about Adonijah making himself king. She realizes that with Adonijah as king everything will change. It means that her relationship with Solomon is in jeopardy, but most of all it means that Solomon's life is in danger. She also fears that Adonijah may take her, as a king has the right to do, and treat her as his property. She already knows from the way Adonijah has made advances toward her that he is a self-absorbed man, like her brothers and other men she knew in her home village. Solomon was so different by comparison, and how she loved him for that. Now she is afraid of being found with Solomon in the gardens in the early morning because things in David's palace are in a state of high alert because of Adonijah's action to make himself king. It will be hard to see who may be in the shadows watching Solomon. David may be having Solomon guarded or Adonijah may be having him watched. She fears what Adonijah would do if he finds out about her love for Solomon.

She feels sad. Were their secret meetings going to end? What did Solomon want to tell her? Did he want to warn her about Adonijah? Maybe he didn't know that she already knew about what Adonijah had done. Or, maybe he had come to tell her he was going to withdraw from her and stop seeing her until the danger was past? Such thoughts caused her to believe they had to stay apart. She wouldn't allow him to risk a conversation with her in the shadows, so she sent him away until daybreak when it would be safer.

ABISHAG continues:

3:1 On my bed night after night I sought him

Whom my soul loves;

I sought him but did not find him. (NASB)

2 I must arise now and go about the city;

In the streets and in the squares

I must seek him whom my soul loves.

I sought him but did not find him. (NASB)

3 The watchmen who make the rounds in the city found me,

And I said, "Have you seen him whom my soul loves?" (NASB)

Solomon had not come back at daybreak. She had waited and waited for him to come, but he had not returned. Now it was night, and she was sleeping in her own bed because David had not called for her. She suspected it was because of the upset caused by Adonijah and that David was dealing with that problem. She heard a rumor that David had made Solomon king, but why wouldn't Solomon have come to her to tell her this? Where was he?

She went over and over matters on her bed that night. Finally, she decided she could wait no longer and went outside to try and find him. She looked first for him in the city in the places they had met before. Maybe he had gone there to hide from his enemies. Maybe she could find someone who had seen him. While searching for him, the watchmen found her; and she inquired of them, but they gave her no help.

3:4

ABISHAG continues:

4 Scarcely had I left them

When I found him whom my soul loves;

I held on to him and would not let him go

Until I had brought him to my mother's house,

And into the room of her who conceived me. (NASB)

After she left the watchmen, immediately she found Solomon.

As happened to Abishag, many watchmen throughout the centuries have not helped women in their quest to find and know God. They have not helped them take care of their inheritance as equals with men. In order for women to move forward in their following of God, they have had to leave such watchmen.

She held Solomon and wouldn't let go until he had come with her to her mother's house.

Possibly her mother had come from Shunem to Jerusalem with Abishag and had secured a house in Jerusalem so that she could be nearby and watch over her daughter's well-being while she was in the palace tending to King David. (See Song 6:9 NET Bible note which says Abishag was the favorite among her mother's daughters.) As such, her mother may well have come with her to Jerusalem. Or maybe Abishag had extended family on her mother's side in Jerusalem. In either case, this could explain why Abishag was able to take Solomon to her mother's house. This may also be where Abishag stayed when David did not need her service, and it may explain how she came to know the daughters of Jerusalem that she refers to often.

Solomon explains to Abishag that he has just returned from Gihon and tells her the story of how David had made him King. She had heard a rumor about this already and had feared that if it was true she would not get to see him again. He tells her his father's health is failing fast, due to the stressful situation with Adonijah. She asks what will happen to Adonijah, and Solomon assures her he will be merciful and let his brother live.

When Solomon tells Abishag, a lowly village woman, in advance of David's death that he has been made the king, this is like Jesus telling the lowly woman at the well that He was the Messiah, the king of the Jews, in advance of His becoming King. The woman at the well was the first person to learn this from Him.

If at this point in the story, Abishag symbolizes the women who were with Jesus before His death, then this whole disturbance around Adonijah could symbolize the problems just prior to the crucifixion of Christ. No doubt, all the women followers of Christ were frightened by the more aggressive actions of the Jewish rulers. The Jewish rulers wanted to be the ones that ruled over the Jews, and so they perceived Jesus' popularity as a threat. They were self-appointed rulers like Adonijah.

Abishag and Solomon began to experience a change in their relationship in the days before David's death because Solomon could not be with her as before. Similarly, the women with Christ began to experience a change in the days leading up to Christ's death when He was no longer able to be with them as before. He had set his face like a flint to obey His Father who was about to make Him King.

The watchman that did not help Abishag symbolize the keepers of the Jewish religion. They did not want anyone following Jesus; therefore, they would never help anyone who was seeking to be with or follow Him. In order to be with Jesus, those who wanted to follow Him had to stop looking to the Jewish leaders and religion-keepers for help and direction.

Solomon, at Abishag's mother's house, tells Abishag that David's rapidly failing health means that she may not be needed in the palace again. It will be harder for him to see her. As king, he will not be as free to come and go, unnoticed, as he had been before. He reassures her of his love for her and tells her he wants to marry her, but it will take time before He can. He needs to go to be with His father and take care of things to prepare the way for marriage to her. David's death is approaching, and the duties of being king are being transferred to him. When David dies, Bathsheba will need time to grieve, so he will have to wait and look for the right time to tell his mother about his love for Abishag. He asks Abishag to wait and to begin to make herself ready for their marriage. She reassures him of her love for him and that she will wait and always be watching for him.

He goes away to return to His father's house and leaves her asleep in her mother's house. He tells her friends, the daughters of Jerusalem, who are lingering outside, not to wake her.

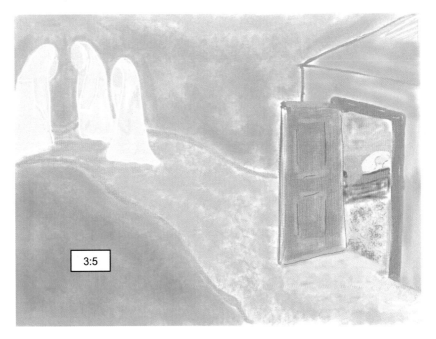

SOLOMON speaks:

5 I adjure you, O daughters of Jerusalem,

By the gazelles or by the hinds of the field,

That you will not arouse or awaken my love

Until she pleases. (NASB)

Chapter 3: A Time of Separation and Deception—Love Grows Cold and Doubt Abounds (Song 3:5–5:1)

A LONG TIME of separation passes.

Let's take a pause for some historical information about Jewish custom:

When the Jewish bridegroom would arrive at the bride's home, he would come for the purpose of establishing a marriage covenant and in order to establish that covenant he had to pay a purchase price....

After the Jewish bridegroom had established the marriage covenant at the bride's home and thereby had obtained his bride to be his wife, he would leave her at her home and would return to his father's house and they would remain separated for a period of time—normally for approximately one year. And during that year of separation the Jewish bridegroom would be busily engaged in his father's house preparing living accommodations to which he could bring his bride later on. (Dolphin)

So Solomon's interaction with Abishag in her mother's house symbolizes Christ espousing himself to his bride.

David dies. Solomon takes his place on the throne of David.

David's death symbolizes Christ's death on the cross, the full payment for His bride. Solomon sitting on the throne symbolizes Christ ascending to the heavenly throne where He has gone away to prepare a place for His bride that she may be with Him.

During the long period that Abishag was separated from Solomon, Adonijah comes to Bathsheba and convinces her to ask Solomon to give him Abishag as a wife. Bathsheba then goes to Solomon. After Solomon tells her he will grant whatever she asks of him, she asks him to give Abishag to Adonijah. Solomon becomes upset. He has made a promise to do whatever she asks of him, and he must keep it. He realizes the only way to save Abishag from marriage to Adonijah is to have Adonijah killed, and he does so.

It is evident that Bathsheba did not know about Solomon's love for Abishag up to this point; because, if she had, she would not have agreed to ask Solomon to give Abishag to Adonijah.

Solomon then tells his mother about the love that he and Abishag have for each other, that he has asked her to marry him, and that he had been waiting for the right time. Bathsheba, who had taken note of Abishag's strong moral behavior with David, had determined long ago that Abishag was a worthy woman of *chayil*. She immediately gives Solomon her blessing on his marriage. Solomon makes things ready and then prepares his palanquin to go to Abishag and tell her it is time for them to marry! That day was the day of the gladness of his heart, the day when his espousal to Abishag received his mother's blessing.

Meanwhile, Abishag's relationship with Solomon and her feelings for him have become damaged by their long time of separation. This separation was keenly felt by her but not by Him. His deep love for her had remained strong, and He had held her close in his heart and thoughts. Abishag's feelings and thoughts as a result of their separation have changed. Her circumstances have affected her adversely, and she has begun to have poor thoughts about Solomon. She can't understand why he had to completely disappear from her life. She longs to see him but can do nothing about it. He has the power to come to her, but he hasn't done so. She has also heard rumors about things he has done as king that trouble her. She has begun to doubt his love.

We have been espoused to Christ, according to Paul (2 Cor. 11:2); however, we still pass through difficult times in which we doubt and do not have the comfort of believing this.

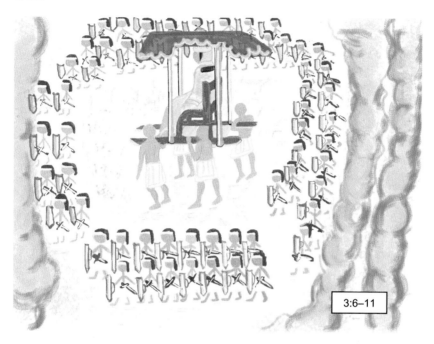

3:6–11

OTHERS speak:

6 What is this coming up from the wilderness

Like columns of smoke,

Perfumed with myrrh and frankincense,

With all scented powders of the merchant? (NASB)

7 Behold, it is the traveling couch of Solomon;

Sixty mighty men around it,

Of the mighty men of Israel. (NASB)

8 All of them are wielders of the sword,

Expert in war;

Each man has his sword at his side,

Guarding against the terrors of the night. (NASB)

9 King Solomon has made for himself a sedan chair

From the timber of Lebanon. (NASB)

10 He made its posts of silver,

Its back of gold

And its seat of purple fabric,

With its interior lovingly fitted out

By the daughters of Jerusalem. (NASB)

11 Go forth, O daughters of Zion,

And gaze on King Solomon with the crown

With which his mother has crowned him

On the day of his wedding,

And on the day of his gladness of heart." (NASB)

One day, Abishag hears this question being raised in the city, "Who is this that comes up out of the wilderness." The king's entourage, his palanquin with sixty valiant men, is coming. She hears that Solomon has been somewhere and is coming back with goodly merchandise. They tell her the news: King Solomon has made all the preparations for his marriage and has been crowned with his mother's blessing to marry. This is the day for which he has waited, and he is exceedingly glad. Everyone is going forth to behold him.

The following provides more information about the Jewish marriage custom:

The Jewish bridegroom at the end of the year of separation would come on an unannounced night to take his bride to be with him. The bride never knew exactly what night he would come. She knew it would be some night near the end of the year of separation but she never knew exactly when. And so on that unannounced night the Jewish bridegroom would call to himself at his father's house his best-man and other male escorts and together those young men would begin a torchlight procession through the streets of the city from the groom's father's house over to the home of the bride.

Here was the bridegroom coming to take his bride to be with him. As those young men would be weaving their way through the streets of the city, bystanders recognizing what was happening, would pick up a shout, "Behold the bridegroom comes." That shout would be carried from block to block to block until finally it would arrive at the bride's home. The major purpose of that shout was to forewarn the bride to the effect that she'd better get ready in a hurry because tonight was the night and her groom was already on his way to take her to be with him.

As soon as she would hear that shout, she sent out word to her bridesmaids to come to her home, get her dressed in her bridal garment and all prepared because this was the night. (Dolphin)

In Song of Songs, at this point, the story is about to take a turn for the worse. When Solomon arrives at her house, it soon becomes apparent that Abishag has a problem with him. She does not respond to him as he had expected. This does not match the Jewish marriage custom! Instead of running to meet him with her bridesmaids, she stays put.

During the long time of separation, Abishag has convinced herself that the worst has happened: Bathsheba would not agree to Solomon marrying her, and Solomon has changed his mind about her. She had feared that becoming king would change him, and it apparently had. As the king, he was doing what men did best: take what they wanted and rule over others. Just last week she had heard, to her great dismay, that Solomon had killed Adonijah! As king, he had the power of death and life, and he had killed his own brother. He had told her he would not do this. This was not the man she knew, the man she had given her heart to. There had been no word from Solomon for so long. She had finally made the decision to leave Jerusalem and return to her valley with her mother who wanted to take her home. Having watched Abishag grieve over Solomon, her mother understood the humiliation her daughter was feeling at having been taken in and fooled by the young prince into believing she was loved, and she wanted to take her daughter home to heal.

Now today's news: Solomon was getting married with Bathsheba's blessing! In her deceived state, Abishag immediately believed he was marrying someone else. This confirmed for her that Solomon had not kept the verbal marriage contract he had made with her. She felt her heart closing completely towards him. She would not let any man into her heart, not now or ever again. She would not allow herself to be hurt again like this.

Suddenly, Solomon appears at her door. She is surprised by this and tries to make sense of it in her mind.

SOLOMON speaks:

4:1 How beautiful you are, my darling,

How beautiful you are!

Your eyes are like doves behind your veil;

Your hair is like a flock of goats

That have descended from Mount Gilead. (NASB)

2 Your teeth are like a flock of newly shorn ewes

Which have come up from their washing,

All of which bear twins,

And not one among them has lost her young. (NASB)

3 Your lips are like a scarlet thread,

And your mouth is lovely.

Your temples are like a slice of a pomegranate

Behind your veil. (NASB)

4:1-5

4 Your neck is like the tower of David,

Built with rows of stones

On which are hung a thousand shields,

All the round shields of the mighty men. (NASB)

5 Your two breasts are like two fawns,

Twins of a gazelle

Which feed among the lilies. (NASB)

Solomon is joyful and ready to tell Abishag the good news that they can marry. First, he breaks forth and begins to describe Abishag from head to foot as was the custom in eastern love poetry (NET Bible Notes). As usual, he speaks directly to her, not about her. He is overwhelmed with his love for her and pours out poetry pointing to all their past times together in the fields, gardens, mountains, and valleys.

This book does not cover the symbolism related to much of the descriptive imagery in the Song, though it is significant. In the related sketch, her hair is like a flock of goats; her neck has bucklers and shields hanging on it like on a tower; her breasts are as two roes; etc. A lot has been written about such imagery and its meaning by others, and the sketch captures some of it. The purpose of this writing, however, is to present a storyline that corresponds with the flow of the Song's language and show its story and meaning from another perspective.

Solomon quickly notices that she is cold and unresponsive. Something is wrong. She says nothing but just stands there. He is taken aback by this and cannot understand what has happened. He remembers his mother's instruction to never impose his wishes on a woman but to always handle her with respect and gentleness.

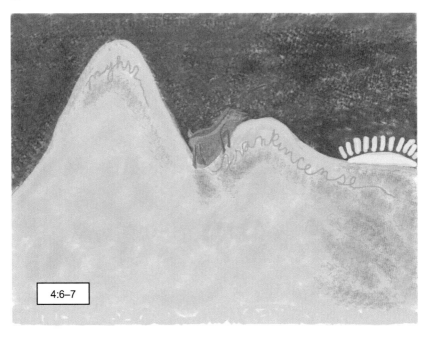

4:6–7

SOLOMON continues:

6 Until the cool of the day

When the shadows flee away,

I will go my way to the mountain of myrrh

And to the hill of frankincense. (NASB)

7 You are altogether beautiful, my darling,

And there is no blemish in you. (NASB)

He soon decides he should leave and go to the mountain of myrrh and the hill of frankincense; but, after he looks at her again and sees how fair she is and that there is no spot in her, he asks her to ...

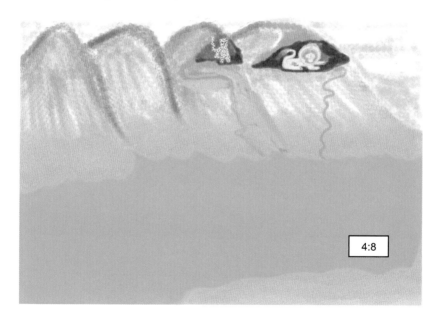

... come away with him.

SOLOMON asks:

8 Come with me from Lebanon, my bride,

May you come with me from Lebanon.

Journey down from the summit of Amana,

From the summit of Senir and Hermon,

From the dens of lions, from the mountains of leopards. (NASB)

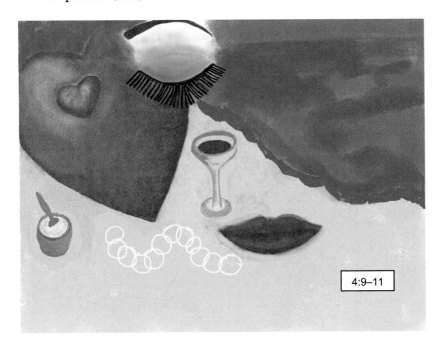

4:9–11

SOLOMON continues:

9 Thou hast ravished my heart, my sister, my spouse;

Thou hast ravished my heart with one of thine eyes,

With one chain of thy neck. (KJV)

10 How beautiful is your love, my sister, my bride!

How much better is your love than wine,

And the fragrance of your oils

Than all kinds of spices! (NASB)

11 Your lips, my bride, drip honey;

Honey and milk are under your tongue,

And the fragrance of your garments is like the fragrance of Lebanon. (NASB)

He tells her how she has ravished his heart with one of her eyes, with one chain of her neck. Her love is better than wine. Her lips drop as the honeycomb; honey and milk are under her tongue.

He has just returned from Lebanon, where he has prepared a place for her, a beautiful garden with orchards and vineyards and spices, and that place is fresh on his mind. But, it is clear: His words are not reaching her.

The real King Solomon had a large vineyard near the mountains of Lebanon, near Shunem, Abishag's village.

SOLOMON continues:

12 A garden inclosed is my sister, my spouse;

A spring shut up, a fountain sealed. (KJV)

13 Your shoots are an orchard of pomegranates

With choice fruits, henna with nard plants, (NASB)

14 Nard and saffron, calamus and cinnamon,

With all the trees of frankincense,

Myrrh and aloes, along with all the finest spices.
(NASB)

15 A fountain of gardens,

A well of living waters,

And streams from Lebanon. (KJV)

He sees her as a garden that is closed, a spring that is not flowing, and a fountain that is sealed. He knows that her heart is like a garden with wonderful spices fed by living waters and streams from Lebanon. It is full of beauty, but it is not open to him. She has shut him out. He departs, knowing he will come and try again later. He will never let her go.

The first problem in the relationship between Abishag and Solomon came as a result of an outward event (Adonijah making himself king), and that event had caused Abishag to have great fear. The problem this time, however, is due to imaginations, thoughts, and doubts in her heart and mind which were formed because of her circumstances and what they spoke to her about Solomon.

After Christ rose from the dead and was crowned King of kings and Lord of lords, a long period of separation between Christ and his believers began. We have been espoused to Christ, yet we don't see Him with our eyes any more. During Christ's centuries-long absence, great hardship has come upon believers and, in particular, upon women, as history shows. Women's love and intimacy with Him through the Spirit came under attack from the devil, who used ungodly Christian leaders to twist the Bible's words in ways that could bring about the lording over and shutting down of Christian women—one of the devil's prime directives. Over time, the mistreatment and oppression of New Testament women served to change their thought about themselves and also their thought about God and how He viewed them. They became a locked garden, a sealed spring, a fountain shut up. Inside each garden, however, "orchard of pomegranates with choice fruits, henna with nard plants, nard and saffron, calamus and cinnamon, with all the trees of frankincense" still flourished.

Abishag is in quite a state when Solomon leaves. She is flooded with thoughts. What? He wants her to go away to the mountains of Lebanon with him. How could he, on the day of his espousals, come to her house and speak to her like this? Does he want her to go to the mountains with him for a fling before he marries? Now that He is king, does he expect to use her like property as his father David had done? Does he expect her to be nothing more than a king's concubine?

Her long separation and nurturing of false thoughts about Solomon have clouded and confused her thinking. She is operating as if things for which she has no evidence are true. Her distrust of Solomon has created a great darkness in her heart and mind concerning him, and this has blinded her to such an extent that she cannot see the obvious.

Abishag gradually admits to herself that Solomon seemed to be made genuinely sad by her coldness. She knows that she still loves him, but she has become convinced that he does not love her, and that she has been deceived by him and his charms. He was very persuasive today, and part of her wanted to respond and be whatever he wanted, be it warming blanket or concubine, but she had been unable to move. She remembers what he said about her being a locked garden and feels sad about that. She wishes she felt differently and that things actually were different.

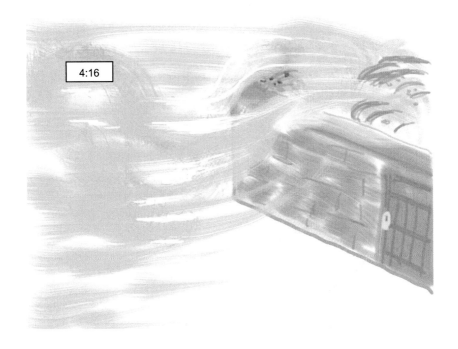

4:16

ABISHAG speaks:

16 Awake, O north wind,

And come, wind of the south;

Make my garden breathe out fragrance,

Let its spices be wafted abroad.

May my beloved come into his garden

And eat its choice fruits! (NASB)

After her new thoughts about him, she whispers a little word to the north wind, almost like a prayer, asking it to come and blow upon her garden and draw her beloved back. Her longing for him has been awakened.

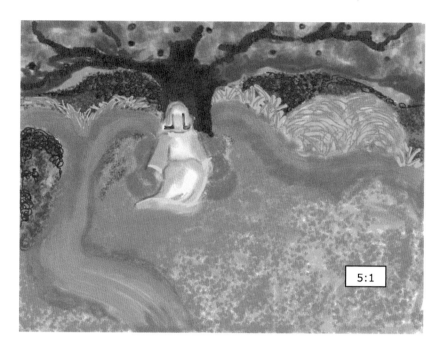

5:1

SOLOMON speaks:

5:1 I have come into my garden, my sister, my bride;

I have gathered my myrrh along with my balsam.

I have eaten my honeycomb and my honey;

I have drunk my wine and my milk.

Eat, friends;

Drink and imbibe deeply, O lovers. (NASB)

The next morning, Solomon is in his own garden, and he speaks aloud to Abishag as if she were there. He is remembering how they used to meet in his garden, and he is longing for her. He had expected her to be as full of joy as he was, and he is still hoping she will change her mind. He decides to go and talk to her again, in the early morning time, like he used to do.

Chapter 4: A Time of Seeking—Love is Stirred (Song 5:2-8)

ABISHAG speaks:

2 I was asleep but my heart was awake.

A voice! My beloved was knocking: (NASB)

SOLOMON speaks:

Open to me, my sister, my darling,

My dove, my perfect one!

For my head is drenched with dew,

My locks with the damp of the night. (NASB)

5:2

ABISHAG speaks:

3 "I have taken off my dress,

How can I put it on again?

I have washed my feet,

How can I dirty them again?" (NASB)

4 My beloved extended his hand through the opening,

And my feelings were aroused for him. (NASB)

5 I arose to open to my beloved;

And my hands dripped with myrrh,

And my fingers with liquid myrrh,

On the handles of the bolt. (NASB)

6 I opened to my beloved,

But my beloved had turned away and had gone!

My heart went out to him as he spoke.

I searched for him but I did not find him;

I called him but he did not answer me. (NASB)

Abishag is asleep, but she wakes up when she hears his voice and his knocking on her door, asking her to open to him. He is wet with dew from his garden. She hears him, but she doesn't respond. She has had a restless night after yesterday's encounter with him. She is still thinking about all that has happened. She wants to leave Jerusalem as soon as she can. She talks to herself, giving excuses for why she cannot go to him. She realizes he wants her to open the door, and she admits to herself how much she wants to do so.

Then suddenly she finds herself on her feet. She goes to open the door, she puts her fingers on the lock, and, with myrrh on her hands, opens the door ... but she was too slow. He is gone. She realizes that her soul was failing within her when she heard his voice. She had felt too weak to respond.

But now, seeing he is gone, she panics. She wants to be with him! She sets out into the city to look for him, calling him, but she can't find him. She cries out to him, but he doesn't answer. She becomes lost wandering in the city in the dark. She is found by the watchmen.

ABISHAG continues:

7 The watchmen who make the rounds in the city found me,

They struck me and wounded me;

The guardsmen of the walls took away my shawl from me. (NASB)

The watchmen were supposed to protect the city of God (Jerusalem) and protect its inhabitants (all of them); but, instead, when she is searching for the one she loves, they beat and wound her. After all, she is a woman out at night—something that is unthinkable, unless she is a prostitute. She had put on a veil to protect herself, but they took it from her.

Once again, she has been abused by men. This time, they were men who were supposed to be God's watchmen against the enemy. This brought back all the memories of her angry brothers. What was she doing? Who could she trust? Solomon had been angry with Adonijah and killed him, his own brother. He had misled her about marriage! Should she risk trusting him again? She had to remember who she was. She was strong and would not let him use her or disrespect her.

5:8

ABISHAG continues:

8 I adjure you, O daughters of Jerusalem,

If you find my beloved,

As to what you will tell him:

For I am lovesick. (NASB)

The daughters of Jerusalem find her, and she tells them all that has happened. As she speaks about Him, her thoughts turn again as she begins to remember that his love was better than wine. She calms as she speaks about him to them, and her emotions swing again to her deepest feelings of love for him—the feelings that caused her to go out searching for him. The daughters can't believe that Solomon could have changed in his love for Abishag. The more Abishag talks about him, something surprising happens. All of a sudden, it dawns on her that all of her poor assessment of him was based on circumstantial evidence. Her actual contact with him had never been anything but wonderful.

Her mind cleared, and she understood. He was telling her the truth when he came to see her. As this light broke on her, the dark, thick, oppressive fog lifted. She understood! The reason he was so happy was because the day that he had promised her would come, had come! He had come to tell her they were to be married soon! How stupid she had been! She remembered the words that had not been able to penetrate. He had said, "My bride ... twice no less!" Oh, how she must have hurt him by her coldness! She remembers again the man she first loved! As she lay there wounded, talking to her friends, she knows he will help her if he learns she has been attacked. In those moments of clarity, she realized that she had allowed lies about him into her mind! She would not allow them to remain! She cast every one of them down and told the daughters, her friends, that if they could find him, she wants them to tell him she has been in travail and is wounded because of her love for him, love which drove her to seek him in the night. She knows he will come to her aid. He still loves her!

Chapter 5: A Time of Deliverance— Love is Restored (Song 5:9-6:11)

OTHERS speak:

9 What kind of beloved is your beloved,

O most beautiful among women?

What kind of beloved is your beloved,

That thus you adjure us?" (NASB)

She feels her joy returning. He did love her, and she did love him! She tells her friends she has made a very big mistake in thinking badly of him. Solomon is the most special of all men. They ask her what her beloved is more than another.

She answers, describing in great detail the handsomeness of the one she loves and why she had risked being hurt to find him.

ABISHAG speaks:

10 My beloved is white and ruddy,

The chiefest among ten thousand. (ASV)

Regarding "white and ruddy," white symbolizes clean, pure, and righteous; while ruddy (or red) could refer to Adam, since the Hebrew word for Adam (Strong's, H120) comes from the Hebrew word for ruddy (Strong's, H119). "White and ruddy" could signify that he is like the last Adam (1 Cor. 15:45) and the first man of the new creation, a new man who is a righteous one!

5:10–16

Abishag's story also symbolizes that of Christians in general and Christian women in particular. Not long after Christ ascended and went to be with His Father, He poured out the Spirit upon the believers and blessed them with every spiritual blessing in the heavenlies. This was His way of being with them and caring for them during their time of separation from Him; but, as time passed, they failed to embrace and learn the way of faith as the way to remain faithful to Him. They let the words He had spoken to them when He was with them slip. They had many thoughts and questions sown into their minds by the devil, who was busy fighting against them. In hard circumstances, he shot fiery darts into their minds, slandering God. Over time, things grew much worse for women, as Satan moved ungodly male Christian leaders to suppress them in the name of God.

What better way to stop the effectiveness of believers on the earth than to turn half of them (male believers) on the other half (female believers). The watchmen who beat Abishag symbolize those male believers who have wounded and oppressed female believers over the centuries since the time Christ rose from the dead.

ABISHAG continues:

11 His head is like gold, pure gold;

His locks are like clusters of dates

And black as a raven. (NASB)

12 His eyes are like doves

Beside streams of water,

Bathed in milk,

And reposed in their setting. (NASB)

13 His cheeks are like a bed of balsam,

Banks of sweet-scented herbs;

His lips are lilies

Dripping with liquid myrrh. (NASB)

14 His hands are rods of gold

Set with beryl;

His abdomen is carved ivory

Inlaid with sapphires. (NASB)

15 His legs are pillars of alabaster

Set on pedestals of pure gold;

His appearance is like Lebanon

Choice as the cedars. (NASB)

16 His mouth is full of sweetness.

And he is wholly desirable.

This is my beloved and this is my friend,

O daughters of Jerusalem. (NASB)

DAUGHTERS speak:

6:1 Where has your beloved gone,

O most beautiful among women?

Where has your beloved turned,

That we may seek him with you? (NASB)

Abishag's words have stirred her friends, the daughters of Jerusalem, to seek him also. They want her to tell them where she thinks they can find him. They want to tell him that Abishag has been hurt so he will come and help her.

ABISHAG speaks:

2 My beloved has gone down to his garden,

To the beds of balsam,

To pasture his flock in the gardens

And gather lilies. (NASB)

3 I am my beloved's and my beloved is mine,

He who pastures his flock among the lilies. (NASB)

6:2

Abishag stops them. She knows exactly where her beloved has gone. He is in his garden, eating fruit and gathering lilies as he always did. The daughters of Jerusalem don't need to find him for her. Yes, she is hurt, but her fresh realization of his love for her has strengthened her. Her love for him will make it possible for her to get to him.

He is waiting for her patiently, as he always did. He is in his garden. When he sees her coming, he is overwhelmed with joy and breaks forth in praise of her. He knew she would get through her inner battle and come back to him. She was too strong, and her love for him, too intense, to become a permanent prisoner of wrong thoughts and feelings about him. Her countenance is completely different than when he last saw her. She had been defeated and cast down, but now her face was lifted up; she was victorious. She was back! The woman he loved had come back to him.

Throughout the long period of separation since Christ ascended to heaven, there have been many Spirit-produced revivals, but these have not yet succeeded in permanently breaking through and defeating the devil. In each of them, Christian women have surfaced and found a measure of freedom and begun to pursue Christ without fear; however, history shows that whenever they did, watchmen beat them.³ Nevertheless, at every visitation by the Spirit, godly women have emerged and become strong and renewed in their love for Christ. Throughout history, because of the enemies warring against them, many strong Christian women have been produced, women who have become expert in warfare against the enemy, able to recognize his lies and cast them down. Their paths made them into women of chayil. They escaped both the neglect and the oppression of the watchmen and found the joy of an intimate love-walk with their beloved Bridegroom on this earth. In their travail, they have brought forth many godly males. They have laid up treasures of faith and love for Him, waiting until He comes again.

---

³ See chapters 4 and 5 of Susan Hyatt's book, *In the Spirit We're Equal*, for what happened during thc carly ccnturies of the church with respect to the Spirit and with respect to the treatment of women. In brief, she shows how Satan used male Christian leaders to produce conditions that shut down two things: the manifest presence of the Spirit and the equal status of Christian women.

SOLOMON speaks:

4 Thou art beautiful, O my love, as Tirzah,

Comely as Jerusalem,

Terrible as an army with banners. (KJV)

5 Turn away thine eyes from me,

For they have overcome me:

Thy hair is as a flock of goats

That appear from Gilead. (KJV)

6:4–10

6 Thy teeth are as a flock of sheep

Which go up from the washing,

Whereof every one beareth twins,

And there is not one barren among them. (KJV)

7 As a piece of a pomegranate are thy temples

Within thy locks. (KJV)

8 There are threescore queens, and fourscore concubines,

And virgins without number. (KJV)

9 My dove, my undefiled is but one;

She is the only one of her mother,

She is the choice one of her that bare her.

The daughters saw her, and blessed her;

Yea, the queens and the concubines, and they praised her. (KJV)

10 Who is she that looketh forth as the morning,

Fair as the moon,

Clear as the sun,

And terrible as an army with banners? (KJV)

Solomon sees Abishag now like the morning sky after a night sky that held the fair moon. Her appearance is like the sun ascending to its high place where it will look down from above over the earth. To him, she is as strong and terrible as an army with banners marching forward into battle.

The NET Bible note says "looking forth" has the meaning of looking down from above as from the sky. This imagery calls to mind the picture of the sign in Revelation 12: a heavenly woman clothed with the sun looking down from on high.

She has withstood the mistreatment of the watchmen and overcome the whispers of the demons in the night lying to her about Solomon, and she is standing upright again. Things are back in a heavenly perspective. He is amazed by this and overcome by her piercing gaze. He tells her how he feels about her new appearance by asking her to turn her eyes away from him because they have overcome him. His father, as a king, had many queens and concubines and virgins for the taking, but for Solomon, she is the only one. She is indeed a woman such as his mother told him to find, a woman of *chayil*.

No type is perfect in all aspects, but the Spirit uses them to teach us. Some suggest that the woman in Song of Songs is Solomon's first love, when he was young and uncorrupted. Later in life, Solomon fell into a bad state and had many wives, some of whom were foreign and corrupted him with their gods (1 Kings 11:1–5). The important thing to remember is that, in Song of Songs, Solomon is a picture of Christ; and Christ is not a type, but the real One, whose purity and love never change!

Chapter 6: A Time To Heal—Another Separation (Song 6:11–13)

6:11–13a

ABISHAG speaks:

11 I went down into the garden of nuts
To see the fruits of the valley,
And to see whether the vine flourished,
And the pomegranates budded. (KJV)

12 Or ever I was aware, my soul made me
Like the chariots of Amminadib. (KJV)

DAUGHTERS speak:

13a Return, return, O Shulammite;

Return, return, that we may gaze at you. (AMP)

After his declaration to her, Abishag knows that, in her wounded condition, she is not yet ready to marry him. She also knows that there are other things she must do to make herself ready, so another time of separation begins; but this one is different because she is free from her doubt and secure in His love and promises. Her faith in him is back, stronger than before. She has been strengthened by the things she has been through. She tells him she needs to return to her home in Shunem for a while to prepare for their marriage. She needs to go back with her mother who is ready to return. She also wants to revisit the vineyards where she was mistreated and see her mother's sons again. She has decided to talk to them about their anger and about their not allowing her to tend her own vineyard. If she is going to make herself ready for her bridegroom, she needs to clear up these things from her past, and she also needs her own vineyard. Solomon agrees she must go and take care of these things. She doesn't ask him the "why" questions in her heart that had plagued her, such as why he killed Adonijah, because she knows one day he will answer them. She trusts him again and will wait. He loves her and is willing to wait for her to make herself ready.

Many times as Christian women, after seeing in a new light our past relationships with angry, neglectful, wounding brothers, we find it necessary to revisit our painful past. As we become new persons in Christ, He leads us to address or set right things that we did not properly address at the time they happened. This is part of making ourselves ready.

When she arrives in Shunem, her princely people, much to her surprise, receive her in chariots. They consider her a person of reputation because she lived in the king's house and took care of King David in his last days. They have heard that she knows King Solomon. They received her like a prince's daughter, not like a vineyard slave.

A good amount of time has passed now, too much time according to the feeling of the daughters of Jerusalem, and they want to see Abishag again. They know that she went home to Shunem to make herself ready. They call out, "Return, return, O Shulamite; return that we may look upon thee."

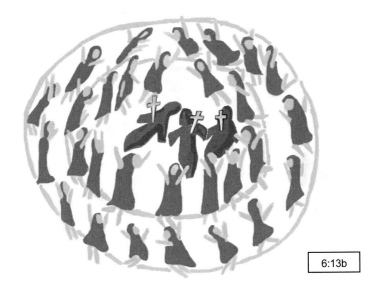

6:13b

WITNESSES speak:

13b Why should you gaze at the Shulammite,

As at the dance of the two armies? (AMP)

This question immediately follows the request for the Shulamite to return.

Commentators have various interpretations of who is speaking in the third-party interjections into Song of Songs. I believe, as some say, that this particular question is asked by heavenly witnesses (such as those in the great cloud of heavenly witnesses mentioned in Hebrews 12) who have a heavenly view of what Abishag has become as she has made herself ready for the king.

The heavenly onlookers answer their own question: "What will you look upon in the Shulamite? ... a dance of two camps." Some translations say armies instead of camps. This part of the verse has numerous translations and interpretations, but this one seems to be the best fit for Abishag at this victorious point in her life.

Contained in this description of Abishag, which is made by the heavenly onlookers, is the culmination of the truth about God's view of women as revealed in Song of Songs. The heavenly onlookers see the big picture. They see in Abishag a symbol of all the women of chayil from the Old Testament (one camp or army) and the New Testament (another camp or army). They see these two armies of females dancing in victory over their enemy!

Chapter 7: A Time of Joy—Together at Last (Song 7:1–8:11)

SUDDENLY, IN SONG OF SONGS, Solomon is with Abishag again. This time, however, he has come to visit her in Shunem, the valley where she lives. He sees that among her people she is being treated like a prince's daughter, not a vineyard slave anymore. Her once angry brothers have acknowledged her as she really is, a woman of *chayil*. She has made herself ready.

7:1a

SOLOMON speaks:

7:1a How beautiful are your feet in sandals,

O prince's daughter! (NASB)

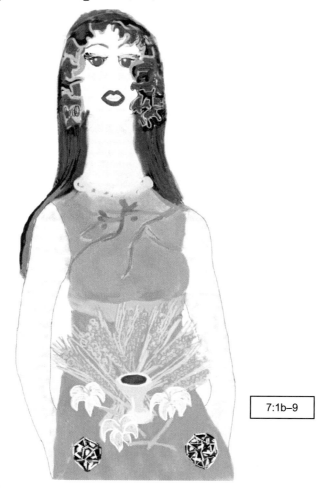

7:1b–9

Solomon is not waiting for Abishag any longer. He has turned himself to come to her and spend time with her as she prepares herself to be his wife. He praises her beauty more, only this time he describes her from her feet to her head.

SOLOMON continues:

1b The curves of your hips are like jewels,

The work of the hands of an artist. (NASB)

2 Your navel is like a round goblet

Which never lacks mixed wine;

Your belly is like a heap of wheat

Fenced about with lilies. (NASB)

3 Your two breasts are like two fawns,

Twins of a gazelle. (NASB)

4 Your neck is like a tower of ivory,

Your eyes like the pools in Heshbon

By the gate of Bath-rabbim;

Your nose is like the tower of Lebanon,

Which faces toward Damascus. (NASB)

5 Your head crowns you like Carmel,

And the flowing locks of your head are like purple
threads;

The king is captivated by your tresses. (NASB)

6 How beautiful and how delightful you are,

My love, with all your charms! (NASB)

7 Your stature is like a palm tree,

And your breasts are like its clusters. (NASB)

8 I said, "I will climb the palm tree,

I will take hold of its fruit stalks."

Oh, may your breasts be like clusters of the vine,

And the fragrance of your breath like apples, (NASB)

9 And your mouth like the best wine!

It goes down smoothly for my beloved,

Flowing gently through the lips of those who fall asleep. (NASB)

7:12

ABISHAG speaks:

10 I am my beloved's,

And his desire is for me. (NASB)

11 Come, my beloved, let us go out into the country,

Let us spend the night in the villages. (NASB)

12 Let us rise early and go to the vineyards;

Let us see whether the vine has budded

And its blossoms have opened,

And whether the pomegranates have bloomed.

There I will give you my love. (NASB)

13 The mandrakes have given forth fragrance;

And over our doors are all choice fruits,

Both new and old,

Which I have saved up for you, my beloved. (NASB)

As he once took her into his gardens, now she brings him to see the fields and villages of her home. She has straightened things out with her brothers and has her own vineyard. It is flourishing. She invites him to see all the pleasant fruits, fruits that she has laid up for him. She is no longer a locked garden, a spring shut up, a fountain sealed. She has opened her heart fully to him and let him make his home in it.

8:1–3

ABISHAG continues:

8:1 Oh that you were like a brother to me

Who nursed at my mother's breasts.

If I found you outdoors, I would kiss you;

No one would despise me, either. (NASB)

2 I would lead you and bring you

Into the house of my mother, who used to instruct me;

I would give you spiced wine to drink from the juice of my pomegranates. (NASB)

3 Let his left hand be under my head

And his right hand embrace me." (NASB)

SOLOMON speaks:

4 I want you to swear, O daughters of Jerusalem,

Do not arouse or awaken my love

Until she pleases." (NASB)

While Solomon is with her in Shunem, she laments to him that, although things have changed considerably, she is still in a situation where she would be despised as a woman (but at least not beaten or put into vineyard labor!) for showing her love to him openly.

She laments that she cannot show her love for Solomon in public and give him a kiss, and wishes that he were her flesh brother so she could do so. Then she would be allowed to take him to her mother's house without anyone disapproving. He could put his left hand under her head and embrace her with his right, without her being looked down upon. She could give him spiced wine of the juice of her pomegranates.

Solomon understands this and knows the future he has planned for her, but the time must be right for him to show her what that is. He warns the daughters of Jerusalem not to interfere.

She is still in a family and religious system where she is treated differently and wrongly because she is a woman, but she is now free in her own person.

8:5

WITNESSES speak:

5 Who is this coming up from the wilderness

Leaning on her beloved?" (NASB)

The question from the on-looking great crowd of heavenly witnesses is: "Who is this coming up from the wilderness leaning upon her beloved?" They are watching Abishag come up from the wilderness with Solomon. Solomon went to get her and is now passing through a wilderness on the way to their destination. She is leaning on him. She is leaving Shunem, her home, where she had her first experiences of being mistreated as a woman. She is going to become Solomon's wife; and, when that happens, all the days of despising, disrespect, and mistreatment will be ended forever. The onlookers ask "who is this" to draw attention to this very important scene.

ABISHAG speaks:

Beneath the apple tree I awakened you;

There your mother was in labor with you,

There she was in labor and gave you birth. (NASB)

6 Put me like a seal over your heart,

Like a seal on your arm.

For love is as strong as death,

Jealousy is as severe as Sheol;

Its flashes are flashes of fire,

The very flame of the Lord. (NASB)

7 Many waters cannot quench love,

Nor will rivers overflow it;

If a man were to give all the riches of his house
for love,

It would be utterly despised. (NASB)

As Solomon and Abishag are traveling, they
remember their former times together, and she reminds
him of coming to wake him up in his garden under the
apple tree, the place that he had told her he was born
and the place where he had been taught by his mother.

*At last, she begins to speak to him directly and
intimately in 2nd person (that is, "you")! Except for one
phrase, early in chapter 1, where she says "your love is
better than wine," she has been reserved, speaking about
him, rather than directly to him. Now she is with him face
to face, and there is nothing separating them. She easily
speaks to him directly as one who is with her and loves
her and treats her as an equal.*

After Solomon tells her the story of what happened
with Adonijah and how Adonijah tricked Bathsheba in
order to take Abishag for his wife, Abishag expresses her
gratitude for his strong-as-death love. She had no idea

such a thing had happened. Now she finally understands why Solomon had to have Adonijah killed.

She is overwhelmed by his love for her when she hears this story. How blessed she is to be loved so greatly! He is, indeed, like no other, the fairest among ten thousand. She had wounded him deeply with her rejection, but he bore her wounds because of his great love for her. He has never spoken poorly about her, not even one word, through all the time of their separation. He always and only spoke well of her. He had remained full of joy knowing his love would prevail, because love never fails.

ABISHAG continues:

8 We have a little sister,

And she has no breasts;

What shall we do for our sister

On the day when she is spoken for? (NASB)

9 If she is a wall,

We will build on her a battlement of silver;

But if she is a door,

We will barricade her with planks of cedar. (NASB)

As they travel together, Abishag is thinking of other women who are still in the perils that she was in before she came to Jerusalem, before she met David and Solomon. She knows that young women need to mature, and she talks to Solomon about them when she says, "we have a little sister that has no breasts."[4] She has been thinking about this and tells him she wants to strengthen women who are inclined already by nature to stand as walls against the enemy. She wants to help them become stronger and build upon them. If they are, by nature, inclined to be an open door to the enemy, she wants to enclose them with protective boards of cedar. She has been both! She has stood strong at times like a wall as she did with David in not becoming his concubine, and she has also let the enemy deceive her and come in through the open door of her mind as she did with lies concerning Solomon. Now she is a free woman, in heart and mind and in circumstance. She understands that all the lessons she has learned will serve her well for the benefit of others. Solomon knows that she will be an excellent queen for the benefit of all in His kingdom.

---

[4] The NET Bible note on this verse says that the brothers of the Shulamite were the ones speaking and that they were making this statement about their little sister Abishag. The note explains the meaning of this verse in terms of Abishag having sex. The translators did not have the concept of Abishag being a woman warrior (a woman of *chayil*) who could have had a little sister that needed to be strengthened as she had been to be a wall against the enemy, or that needed help to become a closed door to the enemy.

8:10

ABISHAG continues:

10 I was a wall, and my breasts were like towers;

Then I became in his eyes as one who finds peace. (NASB)

Abishag, aware that she has become a woman of *chayil,* is no longer self conscious, has no more thought about her dark skin, and she boasts that she is a strong wall for protecting and guarding against the enemy. Her breasts represent her ability to love and jealously fight for people. Such strong love in her heart functions like towers in defense against the enemy. She knows that

Solomon sees her strong love and appreciates her for it. These characteristics have given her great favor in Solomon's eyes. His approval of her shows the kind of man Solomon is, thanks to his mother's teaching. He is not, as some other men, an abuser of strong, capable, helping women, but he is an uplifter of them.

8:11

ABISHAG continues:

11 Solomon had a vineyard at Baalhamon;

He let out the vineyard unto keepers;

Every one for the fruit thereof was to bring a thousand pieces of silver. (KJV)

Abishag had thought they were going back to Jerusalem, but what a surprise! He was taking her to Baal-Hamon, not far from her home in Shunem. Baal-Hamon is not far from Mt. Lebanon[5] and Mt. Hermon. There he had purchased a vast vineyard and prepared a home for her. She remembers earlier when he had come to her and asked asked her to come with him to Mt. Lebanon and Mt. Hermon, and she realizes that he had been referring to his Baal-Hamon garden that he had prepared for her. This is where he was returning from when the daughters of Jerusalem announced his coming up out of the wilderness like pillars of smoke on the day of his espousals.

---

[5] Solomon owned a vineyard in Baal-hamon (possibly Baalbak, or identical with Amana (Conder), situated in the warm and fertile plains of Coele-Syria, overshadowed by the heights of Lebanon Sol 4:8. This vineyard he has let out to tenants etc. (Barnes).

Two Hebrew words are put together in the name of the place where Solomon had his vineyard: "baal" and "hamon." Each has several meanings, and I find the following ones to be very interesting: "Baal" can mean lord or husband (H1167); and "hamon" can mean "noise" or "multitude" (H1995) (Strong's). In the Old Testament, "hamon" is used in 1st Kings 18:41 to describe the noise of a heavy rain; and, in Ezekiel 26:13 to describe the sound of singers; and, in 1st Samuel 4:14 to refer to the tumult of a multitude. Considering these meanings, one might think of the scene in the heavens where the voice of a great multitude is loudly praising God as the sound of many waters (Rev. 19:6).

Chapter 8: A Time of Reaping—Her Very Own Vineyard (Song 8:12-14)

8:12

ABISHAG *continues:*

12 My very own vineyard is at my disposal;

The thousand shekels are for you Solomon,

And two hundred are for those who take care of its fruit. (NASB)

While caring for her own vineyard in Shunem, she had hired her own caretakers. The fruit of her vineyard is now at her disposal. Solomon receives a thousand shekels for the fruit of his vineyard from each caretaker. She has enough fruit in her garden that she declares she will give Solomon a thousand shekels of its proceeds as a free-will offering. She is so well off that she also declares she will give two hundred shekels to the caretakers of her vineyard (rather than take two hundred from them). She is wealthy enough to bless them. She is indeed a woman of *chayil*, honoring both God and man.

8:13

ABISHAG continues:

13 O you who sit in the gardens,

My companions are listening for your voice— ...
(NASB)

Solomon has returned to Jerusalem for a period of time to take care of kingdom matters as his father would expect. He has promised Abishag he will come back to her soon. In Jerusalem, he often sits down (the word "sit" means to sit down, specifically as judge [Strong's, H3427]) in the garden. Friends, companions, and fellows come to hear his voice there, and he gives them his wisdom. His heart is full of love for Abishag, and he speaks of her often as a woman of *chayil*.[6]

---

[6] Ruth 3:11 shows that Ruth was talked about in the gate of the city as being a woman whom all in the city knew to be a woman of chayil, so it is possible that

Solomon also talked about Abishag as such a woman.

8:14

ABISHAG continues:

... Let me hear it! (NASB)

14 Hurry, my beloved,

And be like a gazelle or a young stag

On the mountains of spices. (NASB)

He is gone from her for a period a time, but she remembers every day his promise that he will return to her soon and she will become His bride. Each day she listens for him, longing to hear his voice, and she prays that, like a gazelle or young stag on the mountains of spices, he will make haste and hurry back to her. The mountains surrounding their new home make her think of the mountains of spices that will be produced from the gardens of all those that love Solomon. She knows that there will be mountains of spices for him to enjoy from all the gardens of the women (daughters of Jerusalem, little sisters who mature) whom he will bless and cause to prosper because of their love for him.

She remembers when she first met Solomon how she saw him like a deer on the mountains beckoning her to come with him. She wants other women to learn as she has, to love, trust, and follow the king, a man wonderfully different from all other men. She wants them to know his love as she does. She wants them to become women of *chayil* who can see the enemy coming from afar and defeat him. She wants them to be able to take care of their inheritances and be able to bless others with the fruit of their gardens that are no longer locked, and give them of the water from their springs and fountains that are flowing free.

Spices represent fragrance that is produced from the crushing and curing of fruits, nuts, barks, etc. The overall symbolism in Song of Songs concerning women is profound. By the end of the book, the strong-as death love of Christ has brought woman from a state of slavery and bondage to one of glorious freedom. She is no longer: "a garden enclosed, a spring shut up, a fountain sealed" (Song 4:12). She is no longer one without a vineyard, blackened, bent, and beaten. She is the possessor of her own inheritance, her own vineyard, and is a blessing to others. She is free in every sense of the word. She is a strong, powerful, battle-seasoned, capable woman who is desirous and able to help others be the same. She has an abundance of fruit and spices and wealth. She is no longer separated from Solomon and has been blessed and exalted by him. He, as her husband (espoused), sits (a word that refers to judging) in the garden and is sought after by others for his wisdom. She is able to hear His voice as an equal with Solomon's companions (fellows, men) who listen to his judgment and wisdom.

It is possible that they were espoused and had not yet consummated the marriage, and Solomon left her in the mountain home with her vineyard while he returned to Jerusalem to take care of king's business. In this case, he would have promised her his soon return, and she would have been looking for him upon the mountains of spices. Also, if the Song of Songs woman is indeed Abishag, the case may be that, in God's sovereignty, they actually never married in order to better complete the symbolism of the bride of Christ's long wait for His return.

In Abishag's closing words, calling Solomon to hurry like a deer on the mountains, we can hear a symbolic echo of the prayers of all godly women who have journeyed through much hardship to a place of joy and peace in loving Jesus above all else. They want Him to finish this same work in of all those who love Him. They want Him to enjoy all the fruits and spices that have been grown in the gardens of many hearts because of His longsuffering and faithful love. They pray to hasten the day that He will see the fruit of His cross in full.

It is both fitting and believable that a woman who was brought from slavery into such freedom would compose the most beautiful poetic love song ever written: Song of Songs. And, to repeat, the Song of Songs woman is a woman of chayil! *Let me also repeat that all transformed, godly male believers are included in such a woman, the bride of Christ.*

Chapter 9: A Last Word from Solomon (Prov. 31:10–31)

IF IT IS TRUE that Abishag wrote Song of Songs, then it appears that Solomon, the wisest man that ever lived, by writing Proverbs 31:10–31, may have found the way to have the last word. After all, Christ, of whom Solomon was a type, is both the first and the last. As I read this passage in Proverbs over and over, I couldn't shake the idea that these verses (a specific form of poetry per one commentator) corresponded directly with the Song. The passage appeared to be a description of a woman such as Abishag had become by the end of the Song's story. Near the end of my study on the Song, I discovered a clue that persuaded me that Solomon had written this Proverbs passage *after* Abishag had collaborated with him to write the Song. I found the clue near the end of the passage:

10 Who can find a virtuous [chayil] woman? for her price [is] far above rubies.

11 The heart of her husband doth safely trust in her, so that he shall have no need of spoil.

12 She will do him good and not evil all the days of her life.

13 She seeketh wool, and flax, and worketh willingly with her hands.

14 She is like the merchants' ships; she bringeth her food from afar.

15 She riseth also while it is yet night, and giveth meat to her household, and a portion to her maidens.

16 She considereth a field, and buyeth it: with the fruit of her hands she planteth a vineyard.

17 She girdeth her loins with strength, and strengtheneth her arms.

18 She perceiveth that her merchandise [is] good: her candle goeth not out by night.

19 She layeth her hands to the spindle, and her hands hold the distaff.

20 She stretcheth out her hand to the poor; yea, she reacheth forth her hands to the needy.

21 She is not afraid of the snow for her household: for all her household are clothed with scarlet.

22 She maketh herself coverings of tapestry; her clothing [is] silk and purple.

23 Her husband is known in the gates, when he sitteth among the elders of the land.

24 She maketh fine linen, and selleth [it]; and delivereth girdles unto the merchant.

25 Strength and honour [are] her clothing; and she shall rejoice in time to come.

26 She openeth her mouth with wisdom; and in her tongue [is] the law of kindness.

27 She looketh well to the ways of her household, and eateth not the bread of idleness.

28 Her children arise up, and call her blessed; her husband [also], and he praiseth her.

29 Many daughters have done virtuously [adverb for chayil], but thou excellest them all.

30 Favour [is] deceitful, and beauty [is] vain: but a woman [that] feareth the LORD, she shall be praised.

31 Give her of the fruit of her hands; and let her own works praise her in the gates. (KJV)

The clue I found is in verse 29:

Many daughters have done virtuously [adverb form of *chayil*] but you excel them all!"

All of the verses before and after verse 29 in this passage are written in 3rd person, which would fit with the idea of Solomon objectively writing about what he had learned from his mother about a woman of *chayil*. Then suddenly, in verse 29, Solomon switches to second person and appears to be addressing someone in particular. I believe that, as he wrote all the foregoing verses, he was thinking about Abishag so strongly that he couldn't help but interject this final praise of her by speaking directly to her: "but you excel them all!"

Chapter 10: The Symbolism

THIS INTERPRETATION has not included all of the book's poetic imagery with regards to descriptions of the appearances of the lover and the beloved. It also has not presented the valid, commonly-accepted interpretations with respect to Christ and the church. I wrote it mainly to give God's view of womankind and womankind's journey with Him from Eden to the present, as symbolically shown by the journey of the Song's woman. In so doing, however, I also discovered an astoundingly richer and fuller view of Christ, as symbolized by Solomon.

The Woman (Abishag)

I believe that the woman in the Song symbolizes, concurrently:

- An individual woman

- Women of God throughout time

- The Bride of Christ

In other words, in the Song, the Spirit of God uses inspired poetic writing in telling the story of love between Solomon and a woman. In so doing, God shows us a beautiful, detailed picture of the progressing development of His intense love relationship with mankind through Jesus Christ. At the same time, the Spirit uses this story to show the heart of God toward women, both individually and collectively, acknowledging what they have suffered at the hands of God's enemy for centuries since the time of the fall of mankind and the time of God's pronouncement concerning the role women would play in defeating the devil. It reveals not only God's perfect and tender awareness of the resultant sufferings of women, but also shows God's way of delivering them and maturing them into strong, capable, forceful, and serpent-crushing women of *chayil*. It shows how God ultimately restores them to their rightful position in his plan of full salvation, and, in the latter days of human history, uses them to hasten the second coming of Christ.

This book is pregnant with a spiritual call, in a very real sense, to every believer. That call is to become such a woman, one who is a worthy bride to Christ. This call is to males and females alike. However, it is not possible to understand this book without first having an adjustment made to our concept, our fundamental understanding about males and females, and especially females, so that it matches God's view of them. God's view of both is clearly revealed in Scripture, but His enemy has purposefully concealed and twisted it; in particular, he has perverted God's view of women. He has done so with good reason: Satan hates and fears women and the role God has destined them to play in his removal. When women are in their proper role, the male seed of woman, which Satan fears even more than women, will emerge and finish his judgment.

In his hatred for women, he has produced a plethora of misunderstandings about women, especially in the minds of males. He has put women in a poor light and opened pathways to afflict them. We see this plainly in the historically provable subjugation of women by men, both socially and spiritually. Twisted views of women have become imbedded culturally, socially, and religiously in the psyches of people and have become like cords or bands or even grave clothes which have held and imprisoned believers (both male and female) for centuries. The result is that women who love God have been locked in places of ineffectiveness—ineffectiveness against the enemy of God, the one whom they, by God's design, hate and are destined to defeat through the seed God promised them.

Although Satan has already been dealt the crushing blow by Christ, the male seed of woman, God has not finished putting the enemies of Christ under His feet, as the Bible teaches and our experience shows. The woman has yet to bring forth the Revelation 12 man child (literally, male child). This will take place just before the second coming of Christ (Bushnell, paras. 810–828).

Katharine Bushnell, whom I look forward to thanking in person one day, has, through her writing, unwound my grave clothes and those of my husband. I have watched others have similar experiences when they learn the truth about God's view of women and when that truth begins to set them free.

An Individual Woman

Abishag, in the first symbolic meaning of the woman in the Song, represents an individual woman. Each woman has her own journey to God, but all journeys are similar because of the promise concerning the seed of woman given in the Garden of Eden.

Every woman comes under Satan's hatred when she enters this world by virtue of the fact that God put enmity between the woman and the devil and between woman's seed and the devil's seed. A woman should understand that the devil's hatred is the reason for her having experiences like Abishag's: her brothers' anger, her being used like a slave, her being disrespected and not allowed to take care of her own inheritance, and her skin being blackened because of her brothers' oppression. Satan's hatred is the reason she has been demeaned in ways similar to Abishag, who was not given the right to make her own decisions about her life and future. She was viewed and treated as a beautiful young body that could be used as a warm piece of meat to press against an old man's cold flesh. God's promise to woman, however, that Satan would not prevail, is the behind-the-scenes reason that a woman can find the strength to resist the devil and refuse to be mistreated and misused.

A woman's journey to the place where Christ becomes everything to her is not an easy one. There are tortuous twists and turns throughout a daunting wilderness. There are many encounters with the enemy who wounds her and lies to her; but, as she moves forward by faith in Christ, His steadfast love and overcoming words of blessing teach her to believe in and fully embrace Him. They help her learn about, understand, and lay hold of the freedom He has given her. She discovers that she is not a bondwoman but a free woman, one who is able to bring forth godly seed. She can possess her own inheritance and become a blessing to all around her.

Christ loves each individual woman and he seeks to win the love of each woman by showing her who He is and what He is really like. When her eyes are opened to His true beauty, He succeeds in winning her heart. As a woman's love relationship with Him grows, she begins to discover her particular calling in life with respect to blessing others and bringing forth godly seed. Even though her personal journey is marked with ups and downs, just as Abishag's was in her relationship with Solomon, she keeps moving forward. God's enemy cannot stop her. She becomes more and more a woman of *chayil*, one whom He uses to overcome the devil and hasten the return of Christ.

The daughters, her companions seen throughout the Song, are other women watching. These are women whom God is calling to be like her in her love for Christ and in her resistant stand against God's enemy.

Women of God Throughout Time

In this second symbolic meaning of the woman in the Song, we see that women have suffered under the hatred of the devil throughout history, mostly at the hands of males who are controlled by Satan. However, through a love relationship with Christ into which He draws them by His beauty, tenderness, and kindness, they are freed from oppression, uplifted as female human beings from male-enforced inferiority, and are prepared to fulfill the purpose to which God has called them. As they walk with Him in the freedom He gives them, they help others, especially women, do likewise; and, as they bring Him honor, He also honors them.

"My mother's sons," in Song 1:6, refers, I believe, to fallen males in the line of Cain, the serpent's seed. Cain came out of Eve from her union with Adam when Adam was still unrepentant. He had not repented for blaming Eve and God and for failing to expose the devil. In other words, because of Adam's unrepentant state, Cain became the serpent's seed, as did Cain's descendants. Such fallen men persecute women, especially women who turn back to God. Such men lord it over women and rule over them, making them take care of other vineyards and preventing them from caring for their own. Women have been mistreated by angry males throughout both world and church history. The sun is the heat that comes while tending to another's vineyard and serving another's calling, not one's own. Women have been changed (blackened) by this mistreatment.

Women are aware of their position in worldly and religious society and, at least subconsciously, they are aware of the jeopardy they may find themselves in at the hands of men as they seek to follow the Lord. Many prayers have been prayed for protection, as when Abishag asked Solomon where he fed his flock so that she could avoid the other shepherds' tents, the tents of those who might hurt her (Song 1:8). The Lord always answers such prayers, because He loves them and cares for them.

The section of the Song up to time of the death of David represents the period of time of godly women who were forerunners of Christ. These Old Testament women suffered as Abishag did under the mistreatment of their brothers, men who were living out the fallen Adamic nature, who were of their father the devil (the seed of the serpent). They made women slaves in vineyards, didn't allow them to take care of their own inheritance, blackened their skin by oppression, and demeaned and disrespected them, even treating young virgins as warmers for old men's bodies. They used them as multiple wives and concubines and ruled over them. Yet, these women still pressed forward to become women of *chayil* and brought forth the line of the promised seed until Christ came, born of a woman—one of them. When Christ began his earthly ministry, women traveled with him and ministered to him in the flesh, caring for his material needs. Abishag, in her care for David's flesh, may symbolize these women.

While caring for David, Abishag met Solomon and fell in love with him because of the kind of man he was. This may picture the many women loving Jesus in his earthly ministry because of the kind of man He was—a man like no other they had known. He was not a fallen Adam. He never mistreated them but, rather, treated them with the greatest love and respect. They loved Him in return to such an extent that they sought Him in death and found Him resurrected. Like Abishag, they transitioned from caring for Christ in the flesh to loving Him in resurrection.

The section after Solomon is made king represents the period of time of Christian women who lived after Christ was raised from the dead and made both Lord and Christ by God. These women have suffered, as Abishag did, Satan's intense hatred for women who love Christ, pursue Him, and tell others about Him. They have suffered mistreatment at the hands of the devil, sometimes directly, from flaming arrows of fear and doubt shot into their minds, and sometimes indirectly, through the mistreatment of false religious men—watchmen—who are walking in darkness yet claim to be protectors of God's people.

As with Abishag, such watchmen have not helped women in their quest to find and know Christ and in their desire to take care of their inheritance. Women had to leave such watchmen to move forward in their following of Christ. These watchmen not only failed to help women, they also beat and wounded them when they seemed too aggressive in their pursuit of Christ and were venturing to move outside the accepted cultural norms, as Abishag did when she went out alone in the night to look for the man she loved.

These godly women, though espoused to Christ, and greatly loved by Him during the period of His absence from earth, became, over time, a closed garden, a sealed fountain, and a spring that was shut. Within their gardens, the fruit of their love flourished and grew, but they were private gardens, closed and sealed to others, especially their brothers. Under the long-term suppression by their Christian brothers, some of whom were used by Satan to mistranslate God's words with respect to women,[7] women came to hold a basic misunderstanding of how God saw them. Their intimacy with Christ, who longed to come into their gardens, was negatively impacted. So, even Christ was shut out, limited, from freely enjoying the fruit and spices they produced in their gardens. Abishag symbolizes these women in her withdrawal and her non-responsiveness to her lover's calls. These women are described in Solomon's declaration: "My sister, my spouse, is a garden locked up, a spring shut up, a fountain sealed."

---

[7] See my book, *A Woman of* Chayil; *Far Above Rubies,* for a detailed explanation of this statement. Also, see the same book for explanations about statements in the following paragraphs about Eve turning away from God to Adam and about the male and female characteristics of the bride of Christ.

But also like Abishag, as time approaches for the King to come for his bride, godly Christian women break out of the centuries–old, devil-built strongholds in their minds and rise above the wounding of zealous watchmen by God's grace. Because of Christ's strong persistent love for them and unceasing quest to win them, they find the truth in their beloved's words and see themselves through His eyes. This opens their eyes to the altogether lovely Christ. They want to experience His love and return all the way back to God.

In Eden, Eve as a representative of all women, turned away from God to Adam. Throughout history, women have learned by hard experience what happens when they look to fallen man for their needs: He rules over them. The epitome of fallen man ruling over women is seen in the way they were treated by the kings. (The Bible makes it plain that when the Jews wanted a king, they were rejecting God, saying they did not want to be ruled over by Him but by their fellow men. The Jews got what they wanted, to their detriment.) But when women see Christ, as Abishag saw Solomon, they turn back to Him as their only king. Nothing and no one will be able to stop their intimacy with Him ever again. They proclaim their love for Him. They take care of their own vineyards and are joyful. They lay up an abundance of fruit and give it to Him. They resist the devil with all his wiles and become women whose price is far above rubies, women of *chayil.* They dance before their enemies like two victorious armies (representing both women of the Old Testament and of the New). They tell other women the story of their journey and help them also become women of *chayil.* They rejoice to see Christ sitting in His garden and speaking to all who come to hear Him. They continually hear His voice and love doing so. They call to Him to hasten His coming so He can enjoy the mountains of spices coming from all of the unlocked gardens of the hosts of women whom He has set free to love and serve Him without fear.

Like the women of the Old Testament whose time period peaked with the birth of Christ, the time period of New Testament women will peak with the birth of a large army of godly men, whom the Bible refers to as the "male child." This will be the final fulfillment of God's promise to Eve in the garden. The spiritual seed of woman will take part in the last spiritual battle of this age to make all the enemies of Christ a footstool for His feet.

The Bride of Christ

Abishag, in the third symbolic case, represents the bride of Christ. All of the symbolism explained thus far fits her, only the symbolism goes further.

In Christ, there is neither male nor female (Gal. 3:28), but a new creation (2 Cor. 5:17). Fallen mankind is redeemed to be a new kind of being. This is the bride of Christ. She is the real woman whose price is far above rubies. She is the New Testament's pearl of great price. Paul's characteristics, as described in Acts 20 (including humility of mind), show that he was becoming part of such a "woman." In order to understand the symbolism in the Song with respect to the bride of Christ, one must see this new creation, a bride, who is referred to as a woman in the sense that she is a counterpart to Christ. Her characteristics are both male and female, but not male and female according to our fallen understanding or experience of the two genders (where males rule over females, and females enable males to live in their old sinful natures). Her characteristics are male and female as God sees these roles:

Women have the freedom Christ gave them through redemption, the same freedom He gave men, to follow Him as their only Lord and Master.

Women are in their role to help men come back to lives of full dependence on Christ by praying for them and speaking the truth to them in love.

Men treat women with respect and honor and value them as equals in their spiritual journey to know Christ.

Men accept the help God gives to them through women.

Both men and women stand as one new creation, not male or female, to war against God's enemy by faith and to love Christ with all their hearts.

During her journey through the wilderness of this world, the bride of Christ becomes strong, capable, and powerful—able to do battle with the enemy (male-like qualities). At the same time, she becomes nurturing, loving, and able to bring forth godly seed. She is rich in love and good works and able to give of her riches to others. In these roles, she is fully dependent on God as Jesus showed He was every day of his earthly journey (female-like qualities). She matches Him perfectly because she came out of Him. Above all else, she loves Him. She is full of praise and adoration for Him, as He is for her. At the end of the Song, the free and joyful woman, the bride, is calling for Christ to make haste to come. This corresponds to the book of Revelation where the Spirit and the bride say, "Come" (Rev. 22:17). Also, at the end of the Song, the woman who is "fair as the morning, clear as the sun," points us to the woman in Revelation 12, a sign in the heavens, clothed with the sun, the moon under her feet, a crown of stars on her head. She is laboring to bring forth the man child. Also, at the end of the Song, the woman coming up from the wilderness seems to represent the women of *chayil* in both the Old Testament and New Testament, because she is described as a dance of two armies.

Having become new creation beings, Christians are on a journey as described above in "An Individual Woman." This woman, as a symbol of the body of Christ, also includes male believers, believers who are also hated and persecuted by Satan because they are pursuing Christ. In fact, the "male" side of the new creation is actually what is called the "seed of woman." In other words, the seed of woman referred to in the Genesis promise is male. Christ was male. The Revelation child to come is male. The male side of creation represents the ability to do battle, to war and, as Genesis says, to "subdue the earth and conquer it," taking it back from the prince of this world who has been judged by Christ. Woman produces the seed of woman through her relationship with God—the seed who is a conquering male, bold and strong with great humility, as seen in Christ. The woman's spiritual warfare gives spiritual birth to a body of conquering males, warriors who will finish the charge given in the Garden of Eden to subdue and conquer the earth. These males are actually more feared than women, because Revelation indicates that they will be directly involved in carrying out the final judgment on the devil.

So in the Song, allegorically, we see the development of this wonderful being, the bride of Christ, a new creation who will bring an end to this age and usher in the next. The bride, the Lamb's wife in Revelation 21, is the end product! After all the work is done, the Lamb will marry the woman He has loved, carried, and nurtured—the woman made up of those who followed Him wherever He went. She is, in God's eyes, a "woman," a new creation, one who came from both male and female beings of the fallen creation. She is a free "woman." She has the male and female characteristics that were created by God before the fall when man was made in God's image. This free woman is a woman of *chayil* as described in Proverbs 31:10–32. Her price is that of a pearl of great price—a price far above rubies. She is so valuable that Christ sold all He had and bought her.

In the end of Revelation, Christ comes to earth with her and dwells with her. There will be a new heaven and new earth—a vast garden—where all the old things are passed away and all things are become new.

The Man Solomon

In the Song, Solomon represents Jesus Christ. Matthew 1:1 says that Jesus Christ is the son of David (Solomon). Jesus said concerning Solomon, a type of Christ, "a greater than Solomon is here," referring to Himself. Jesus was the fulfillment of the type of Solomon, who was the wisest man who ever lived until, of course, Jesus, who is greater and wiser than Solomon.

Upon completing my interpretation of the Song, what stood out to me most of all was the brilliant view of Christ and his love for all of His people as seen through Solomon's love for Abishag. We learn about Solomon's character, and therefore learn more about Christ, in two ways in the Song: (1) by seeing how he treats Abishag and how he speaks about her, and (2) by considering what he did behind the scenes on her behalf. One translation of Song of Songs 1:3 is, "No wonder the young women adore you!" Only a woman who has been treated most excellently by a most excellent man could speak like this. Solomon pictures the most excellent love of the only man who is truly capable of evoking such a response of love from those He loves: Jesus is the One whom we see in Solomon's excellent behavior. Solomon treated Abishag with great kindness and respect. He was an excellent man, full of joy and well speaking. He was a longsuffering lover of a lowly, abused woman. He patiently wooed her until she finally decided to let him kiss her.

Jesus treated women with great respect and love. He showed them how He valued them. And, oh, how they loved him! Mary, an absolutely yielded woman, was His mother and the means for Him to have a body of flesh so that He could fulfill his Father's will. God honored Mary by coming to her, an uneducated, lowly, suppressed Jewish woman, and giving her the invitation to bring forth the godly seed that was promised at the time of Adam and Eve's fall. When Jesus began his ministry, women traveled with Him and gave of their wealth to care for Him. Mary sat at his feet and was taught God's Word, something Jewish women were not allowed to do. A sinful woman whom He saved anointed his feet with costly oil and tears, and wiped them with her hair. He released a woman from her oppressive infirmity which had bowed her body and crippled her walk for eighteen years. He spoke to a woman in public by a well, in defiance of the Jewish oral law. He answered the prayers of two women for their dead brother. No man of that day treated or affected women like Jesus did.

In the Song, we also see symbolism about our rescue from the devil. In order for Abishag to successfully make it through her battles and finish her journey, Solomon had to stop Adonijah when he tried to steal the throne, and he had to completely destroy Adonijah when he tried to take Abishag for his own wife. Solomon's love, strong as death, worked until Abishag was a free woman, had her inheritance back, and she could bless others. His longsuffering love made it possible for her to make herself ready as his bride who was waiting for his return.

Adonijah symbolizes the devil, who tried to usurp the throne of God and who, through trickery and craftiness, seduced mankind in the Garden of Eden, seeking to take away God's people for himself. Just as Solomon killed Adonijah, Christ destroyed the devil on the cross and freed us from our bondage to him. He blessed us in heavenly places and made us capable of blessing others. His longsuffering love made it possible for us to make ourselves ready to be His bride and wait eagerly for His return.

We also see something about Christ in Solomon's attitude toward women when compared with Adonijah's attitude toward women. Solomon treated his mother, Bathsheba, with the greatest respect and honored her with a queen's seat when she came to see him. He also honored her by telling her that he would give her whatever she asked of him—even before she had made her request. Adonijah, on the other hand, saw Bathsheba as someone he could use for his own ends. He also saw Abishag as property he could gain for himself by trickery.

There is a noteworthy difference between Solomon and Adonijah: their mothers. The difference in the mothers may account for the difference in the sons. Adonijah's mother was named Haggith. She was a woman who was basically held in bondage in King David's harem. She was not free to do as she pleased, but had to live only to please the king. In this sense, her son, Adonijah, could be considered to be the son of a bondwoman.

I believe that Solomon's mother, Bathsheba, was a different kind of wife to David. She had become David's wife through atypical channels, though none less demeaning than how other women had become his wives or concubines. We can tell by what Bathsheba taught Solomon, and by what Solomon wrote in Proverbs 31, that she passed on to him a different view of women than what was held commonly in the culture of the day. I believe this indicates David's relationship with her was different than his relationship with his other wives. This was possibly due to their painful history together, when they suffered the death of their child because of God's judgment. Later, because of Bathsheba's vows to God (Prov. 31:2) concerning her second child Solomon, she may have stood up to David and obtained the freedom to instruct her son as she pleased. The way for him to give her this freedom was open because of David's sin and subsequent repentance for what he had done. He had not only sinned against Uriah, her husband, he had sinned against Bathsheba, misusing his position as king. He had ruled over her. It is easy to see that he would have given her freedom in this matter. The fact that she made a vow or vows to God also speaks to her being free. So, one might say that Solomon was born of a free woman and brought up by a woman of *chayil*. This gives us an explanation for why he was an excellent man who had an excellent relationship with his mother and with Abishag. Solomon, as seen in the Song, portrays for us the truth that Christ has set both men and women free so they can each be in a right relationship with God. As Bushnell says:

> Thousands of Christians, held in bondage by human companions, are crying out for a clearer realization of covenant relations with God, and God's demand is ever the same: "Let my people go, that they may serve me." God may remember His covenant with our fathers, but nevertheless we are NEVER in full covenant relations with Him until FREE. And this applies to women as well as men. The freedom or bondage of the mother, moreover, both Sarah and St. Paul declare, shall determine the status of the son. No son of a bondwoman, because of her spirit in him, can, as such, enter into full covenant relations with God. Fathers of sons, who hold their wives in sensual bondage, doom those sons to a personal sensual bondage. It is God's own law then, that one sex cannot get free and the other sex remain in bondage. It is impossible to understand the

enormous extent to which all Christendom has been morally crippled in its progress by the attempt to keep the female sex in bondage, especially to the husband's sensuality. (Bushnell, para. 303)

The Song: Our Love Story

As we see in Abishag's story with Solomon, God's way is to allow us to grow strong through suffering and difficulties, with only our faith in Him and His promises to sustain us. He respects our freedom (His gift to us) to make our own choices. Measured sufferings help us learn to make the right ones. He has the power to intervene at any point and remove our afflictions, but when it is in our best interest not to do so, He doesn't. He can prevent watchmen from wounding us, but if it is for our long-term, highest good, He doesn't. He can easily end our time of separation from Him, but because such separation will work good for us, He doesn't. He wants us to learn to choose rightly and to want what we should want—Him. He patiently works with us and waits for us to learn this.

God has given us His sure promises. He is allowing us to learn to use them, empowered by His grace, to fight the enemies in our mind and in our environment. He is letting us learn how to stand up to our angry brothers. He is letting us learn how to obtain and care for our own vineyards and gardens and learn how to grow fruit, make fragrant spices, and lay up riches and blessings for Him and others. Eventually, Abishag became so beautiful to Solomon in all her victorious ways, and the fragrance coming from her garden became so overwhelming, that he could no longer resist her and he came for her! This, too, will be our end with our heavenly King!

At this point, it is fitting to say that by the time Christ comes for us as His bride, we will all, both male and female believers who have loved and pursued Him, be His amazing woman of *chayil!* In Christ, there is neither male nor female, but a new creation, created in Christ Jesus!

Song of Songs is the story of Jesus and each and every believer! Now, just how wonderful is that! It is the story of millions of little Abishag's making themselves ready to be His bride!

Here are some of the treasures in this book that each one of us can walk in everyday:

- Jesus is always waiting for each one of us to invite him to kiss us, morning, noon, and evening.

- Jesus is the One who is always ready to speak directly to each one of us when we ask and listen. We are the ones who are prone to hold Him at a distance, speaking about Him, instead of to Him.

- Jesus has nothing but good things, even wonderful things, to say about each one of us, because He knows the end of our story.

- Jesus has taken away the throne from the devil who tried to be king and rule over each one of us.

- Jesus destroyed the devil who wanted to have each one of us for himself and keep us from marrying Christ.

- Jesus has called each one of us to be a warrior (part of an army) who overcomes the evil one by having faith in every battle.

- Jesus is the husband of multitudes; and, right now, He is preparing a place for each one of us to come and dwell with Him for eternity.

- When our love grows cold through fear and doubt and other such, His stays hot! We may forget Him, but He doesn't forget us, not even for a second.

- Jesus has left us with all His promises and is letting each one of us learn that they are trustworthy.

- Jesus doesn't rescue us from trials until they have done their work to make each one of us a strong woman of chayil.

- Jesus is determined for each one of us to realize the truth that our vineyard is ours, that we can take care of it, and that we can bless others through it. He does not want us to be left as a garden enclosed, a spring shut up, a fountain sealed.

- Jesus wants each one of us to wait and watch for him every day and even to hasten His appearing.

Appendix: A More Thorough Exposition of the Biblical Support for My Background Story

Solomon's Mother's Influence

1 ... the oracle which his mother taught him:

2 What, O my son?

And what, O son of my womb?

And what, O son of my vows? (NASB)

These verses show us that the wisdom found in Proverbs 31 was taught to Solomon by his mother, Bathsheba. They also show us that she made some kind of vows concerning him. Maybe her vows were about how she would bring him up and what she would teach him. I still remember how shocked I was on a day in 2010 when it dawned on me that the source of the description of what many today call the "Proverbs 31 woman" was Bathsheba! Bathsheba, a woman who had committed adultery with David, was the source of the description of a woman of *chayil,* a woman whose price is far above rubies!

Bathsheba was brought to King David after he saw her bathing on her roof. Apparently, she had no say in whether she came or not. She submitted to him, and the unintended result was that she had a child. Then, David had her husband killed. Later, when David came under God's judgment for these sins, David repented. It is most likely that Nathan's confrontation of David also caused Bathsheba great shame and sorrow, and that the loss of their child brought her inconsolable grief that led to her own repentance. The fact that God gave them another son, Solomon, is evidence of both of their repentances and God's forgiveness.

Bathsheba had been a victim of the king's lust and also of her own weakness. Some may say she knew he could see her bathing on the roof and that she sought to attract him; however, the Bible does not say or indicate this. Rather, it says that David saw her, sent for her, and that he had his way with her. He was the king of Israel, a great and powerful man, and she came under his kingly aura. In light of their adultery and David's subsequent murder of her husband, and in light of the death of her first child, she may have realized she had been a weak and cowardly woman who had showed no strength or power in the face of temptations. She may have realized that she should have stood up to David and said, "No." She could have done so because God's Word, which forbade adultery, was on her side. Had she stood up to him, she might have been used by God to convict David's conscience and prevent him from committing adultery and the subsequent murder.

At any rate, the contents of Proverbs 31:10–31 show us that Bathsheba had come to appreciate a woman who was strong, capable, and even assertive in matters of right and wrong; and, she had taught her son to value this kind of woman, a woman of *chayil*. Her teaching reveals that she did not want her son to disrespect women or lust after them and take advantage of them, as David had done with her. No doubt, she would have wanted her son to find a wife that was the kind of wife she should have been to Uriah and, by God's mercy and through His forgiveness, she had now become to David.

Adonijah Exalts Himself to Be King

Right after Abishag came to the palace as described in 1st Kings 1:1–4, verse 5 tells us that Adonijah, Solomon's older half brother, exalted himself to be king:

5 Now Adonijah the son of Haggith exalted himself, saying, "I will be king." So he prepared for himself chariots and horsemen with fifty men to run before him. 6 His father [David] had never

crossed him at any time by asking, "Why have you done so?" And he was also a very handsome man, and he was born after Absalom. 7 He had conferred with Joab the son of Zeruiah and with Abiathar the priest; and following Adonijah they helped him. 8 But Zadok the priest, Benaiah the son of Jehoiada, Nathan the prophet, Shimei, Rei, and the mighty men who belonged to David, were not with Adonijah. 9 Adonijah sacrificed sheep and oxen and fatlings by the stone of Zoheleth, which is beside En-rogel; and he invited all his brothers, the king's sons, and all the men of Judah, the king's servants. 10 But he did not invite Nathan the prophet, Benaiah, the mighty men, and Solomon his brother. (1 Kings 1:5–10, NASB)

When Adonijah realized the time of David's death was nearing, he influenced some of David's men to follow him and to crown him king. He invited all his brothers to his exaltation but excluded, among others, his brother Solomon and the prophet, Nathan.

Nathan Warns Bathsheba About Adonijah

11 Then Nathan spoke to Bathsheba the mother of Solomon, saying, "Have you not heard that Adonijah the son of Haggith [one of David's wives] has become king, and David our lord does not know it? 12 So now come, please let me give you counsel and save your life and the life of your son Solomon. 13 Go at once to King David and say to him, 'Have you not, my lord, O king, sworn to your maidservant, saying, "Surely Solomon your son shall be king after me, and he shall sit on my throne? Why then has Adonijah become king?"' 14 Behold, while you are still there speaking with the king, I will come in after you and confirm your words." (1 Kings 1:11–14, NASB)

Bathsheba Goes to David About Adonijah

In the following, note that Abishag was present for the conversation in which Bathsheba told David about Adonijah having made himself king. Abishag heard that Bathsheba thought Adonijah might do away with her and with Solomon:

> 15 So Bathsheba went in to the king in the bedroom. Now the king was very old, and Abishag the Shunammite was ministering to the king. 16 Then Bathsheba bowed and prostrated herself before the king. And the king said, "What do you wish?" 17 She said to him, "My lord, you swore to your maidservant by the LORD your God, saying, 'Surely your son Solomon shall be king after me and he shall sit on my throne.' 18 Now, behold, Adonijah is king; and now, my lord the king, you do not know it. 19 He has sacrificed oxen and fatlings and sheep in abundance, and has invited all the sons of the king and Abiathar the priest and Joab the commander of the army, but he has not invited Solomon your servant. 20 As for you now, my lord the king, the eyes of all Israel are on you, to tell them who shall sit on the throne of my lord the king after him. 21 Otherwise it will come about, as soon as my lord the king sleeps with his fathers, that I and my son Solomon will be considered offenders." (1 Kings 1:15–21, NASB)

Nathan Goes to David About Adonijah

> 22 Behold, while she was still speaking with the king, Nathan the prophet came in. 23 They told the king, saying, "Here is Nathan the prophet." And when he came in before the king, he prostrated himself before the king with his face to the ground. 24 Then Nathan said, "My lord the king, have you said, 'Adonijah shall be king after me, and he shall sit on my throne?' 25 For he has gone down today and has sacrificed oxen and fatlings and sheep in abundance, and has invited

all the king's sons and the commanders of the army and Abiathar the priest, and behold, they are eating and drinking before him; and they say, 'Long live King Adonijah!' 26 But me, even me your servant, and Zadok the priest and Benaiah the son of Jehoiada and your servant Solomon, he has not invited. 27 Has this thing been done by my lord the king, and you have not shown to your servants who should sit on the throne of my lord the king after him?" (1 Kings 1:22–27, NASB)

David Had Solomon Crowned King

28 Then King David said, "Call Bathsheba to me." And she came into the king's presence and stood before the king. 29 The king vowed and said, "As the LORD lives, who has redeemed my life from all distress, 30 surely as I vowed to you by the LORD the God of Israel, saying, 'Your son Solomon shall be king after me, and he shall sit on my throne in my place'; I will indeed do so this day." 31 Then Bathsheba bowed with her face to the ground, and prostrated herself before the king and said, "May my lord King David live forever."

32 Then King David said, "Call to me Zadok the priest, Nathan the prophet, and Benaiah the son of Jehoiada." And they came into the king's presence. 33 The king said to them, "Take with you the servants of your lord, and have my son Solomon ride on my own mule, and bring him down to Gihon. 34 Let Zadok the priest and Nathan the prophet anoint him there as king over Israel, and blow the trumpet and say, 'Long live King Solomon!' 35 Then you shall come up after him, and he shall come and sit on my throne and be king in my place; for I have appointed him to be ruler over Israel and Judah." 36 Benaiah the son of Jehoiada answered the king and said, "Amen! Thus may the LORD, the God of my lord the king, say. 37 As the LORD has been with my lord the king, so may He be with Solomon, and

make his throne greater than the throne of my lord King David!"

38 So Zadok the priest, Nathan the prophet, Benaiah the son of Jehoiada, the Cherethites, and the Pelethites went down and had Solomon ride on King David's mule, and brought him to Gihon. 39 Zadok the priest then took the horn of oil from the tent and anointed Solomon. Then they blew the trumpet, and all the people said, "Long live King Solomon!" 40 All the people went up after him, and the people were playing on flutes and rejoicing with great joy, so that the earth shook at their noise. (1 Kings 1:28–40, NASB)

Adonijah Is Spared

41 Now Adonijah and all the guests who were with him heard it as they finished eating. When Joab heard the sound of the trumpet, he said, "Why is the city making such an uproar?" 42 While he was still speaking, behold, Jonathan the son of Abiathar the priest came. Then Adonijah said, "Come in, for you are a valiant man and bring good news." 43 But Jonathan replied to Adonijah, "No! Our lord King David has made Solomon king. 44 The king has also sent with him Zadok the priest, Nathan the prophet, Benaiah the son of Jehoiada, the Cherethites, and the Pelethites; and they have made him ride on the king's mule. 45 Zadok the priest and Nathan the prophet have anointed him king in Gihon, and they have come up from there rejoicing, so that the city is in an uproar. This is the noise which you have heard. 46 Besides, Solomon has even taken his seat on the throne of the kingdom. 47 Moreover, the king's servants came to bless our lord King David, saying, 'May your God make the name of Solomon better than your name and his throne greater than your throne!' And the king bowed himself on the bed. 48 The king has also said thus, 'Blessed be the

LORD, the God of Israel, who has granted one to sit on my throne today while my own eyes see it.'"

49 Then all the guests of Adonijah were terrified; and they arose and each went on his way. 50 And Adonijah was afraid of Solomon, and he arose, went and took hold of the horns of the altar. 51 Now it was told Solomon, saying, "Behold, Adonijah is afraid of King Solomon, for behold, he has taken hold of the horns of the altar, saying, 'Let King Solomon swear to me today that he will not put his servant to death with the sword.'" 52 Solomon said, "If he is a worthy man, not one of his hairs will fall to the ground; but if wickedness is found in him, he will die." 53 So King Solomon sent, and they brought him down from the altar. And he came and prostrated himself before King Solomon, and Solomon said to him, "Go to your house." (1 Kings 1:41–53, NASB)

David Dies

10 Then David slept with his fathers and was buried in the city of David. 11 The days that David reigned over Israel were forty years: seven years he reigned in Hebron and thirty-three years he reigned in Jerusalem. 12 And Solomon sat on the throne of David his father, and his kingdom was firmly established. (2 Kings 2:10–12, NASB)

Adonijah Tries To Take Abishag as His Wife

13 Now Adonijah the son of Haggith came to Bathsheba the mother of Solomon. And she said, "Do you come peacefully?" And he said, "Peacefully." 14 Then he said, "I have something to say to you." And she said, "Speak." 15 So he said, "You know that the kingdom was mine and that all Israel expected me to be king; however, the kingdom has turned about and become my brother's, for it was his from the LORD. 16 "Now I am making one request of you; do not refuse me."

And she said to him, "Speak." 17 Then he said,
"Please speak to Solomon the king, for he will not
refuse you, that he may give me Abishag the
Shunammite as a wife." 18 Bathsheba said, "Very
well; I will speak to the king for you." (1 Kings
2:13–18, NASB)

This is a most curious piece of information given to
us by God. Why does the Holy Word tell us that Adonijah
wanted to marry Abishag and that he went about getting
her by using Solomon's mother? Adonijah knew that
Solomon would not deny his mother whatever she asked
and that he would have to give Abishag to him. What
happens next lets us realize the very great possibility that
Solomon himself loved Abishag.

Adonijah Is Executed by Solomon

19 So Bathsheba went to King Solomon to speak
to him for Adonijah. And the king arose to meet
her, bowed before her, and sat on his throne;
then he had a throne set for the king's mother,
and she sat on his right. 20 Then she said, "I am
making one small request of you; do not refuse
me." And the king said to her, "Ask, my mother,
for I will not refuse you." 21 So she said, "Let
Abishag the Shunammite be given to Adonijah
your brother as a wife." 22 King Solomon
answered and said to his mother, "And why are
you asking Abishag the Shunammite for
Adonijah? Ask for him also the kingdom—for he
is my older brother—even for him, for Abiathar
the priest, and for Joab the son of Zeruiah!"
23 Then King Solomon swore by the LORD,
saying, "May God do so to me and more also, if
Adonijah has not spoken this word against his
own life. 24 Now therefore, as the LORD lives, who
has established me and set me on the throne of
David my father and who has made me a house
as He promised, surely Adonijah shall be put to
death today." 25 So King Solomon sent Benaiah

the son of Jehoiada; and he fell upon him so that
he died. (1 Kings 2:19–25, NASB)

Solomon spared Adonijah when he tried to steal the
kingdom from him; but, when Adonijah tried to take
Abishag for his wife, Solomon had him killed!

Adonijah had backed Solomon into a corner. Solomon
had promised to give his mother whatever she asked, so
he was bound by his word to give Abishag to Adonijah.
The fact that Solomon immediately ordered the death of
Adonijah speaks to the great possibility that Solomon
loved Abishag himself and wanted to marry her. The only
way he would not have to give Abishag to Adonijah was if
Adonijah was dead, so he had him killed. This gave
Solomon a way out of having to break his word to his
mother, and it also saved Abishag from this marriage.

For love is strong as death;

Jealousy is cruel as Sheol; (Song, 8:6b, ASV)

Bibliography

"Barnes' Notes on the Bible." From Bible Hub, Parallel Commentaries. 2016. http://biblehub.com (accessed September 17, 2016).

Dolphin, Lambert. "Love and Relationships: Song of Solomon." 2005. http://ldolphin.org/relationships.html (accessed October 18, 2016).

"Strong's Definitions." From Blue Letter Bible. 2016. https://www.blueletterbible.org (accessed October 19, 2016).

Websites Used for Bible Verses

BibleGateway. https://www.biblegateway.com.

Bible Hub. http://biblehub.com.

Blue Letter Bible. https://www.blueletterbible.org.

Made in the USA
Middletown, DE
10 January 2023

21757011R00069